Beatty:

Frontier Oasis

Beatty:
Frontier Oasis

Robert D. McCracken

Nye County Press
TONOPAH NEVADA

BEATTY: FRONTIER OASIS
by Robert D. McCracken

Published in 1992 by Nye County Press
Nye County Commissioners
Tonopah, Nevada 89049

Layout by Polly Christensen, Longmont, Colorado

Printed in the United States of America

Library of Congress Catalog Card Number: 90-060856
ISBN: 1-878138-55-3

To the memory of Bob Montgomery and all desert
prospectors who dreamed of making the big strike

In appreciation for their unwavering support and encouragement for the Nye County Town History Project:

Nye County Commissioners

Robert "Bobby" N. Revert
Joe S. Garcia, Jr.
Richard L. Carver
Barbara J. Raper
Dave Hannigan
Joe Maslach
Cameron McRae

and Nye County Planning Consultant

Stephen T. Bradhurst, Jr.

Contents

Preface

Historians generally consider the year 1890 as the close of the American frontier. By then, most of the western United States had been settled, ranches and farms developed, communities established, and roads and railroads constructed. The mining boomtowns, based on the lure of the overnight riches from newly developed lodes, were but a memory.

Nevada was granted statehood in 1864, but examination of any map from the late 1800s shows that although much of the state was mapped and its geographical features named, a vast region—stretching from Belmont south to the Las Vegas meadows, comprising most of Nye County—remained largely unsettled and unmapped. In 1890 most of southcentral Nevada remained very much a frontier, and it continued to be so for at least another twenty years.

The great mining booms at Tonopah (1900), Goldfield (1902), and Rhyolite/ Beatty (1904) represent the last major flowerings of what might be called the Old West. Consequently, southcentral Nevada, notably Nye County—perhaps more than any other region of the West—remains close to the American frontier. In a real sense, a significant part of the frontier can still be found there. It exists in the attitudes, values, lifestyles, and memories of residents. The frontier-like character of the area is also visible in the relatively undisturbed condition of the natural environment, most of it essentially untouched by humans.

Aware of Nye County's close ties to our nation's frontier past and the scarcity of written sources on local history (especially after about 1920), the Nye County Board of Commissioners initiated the Nye County Town History Project (NCTHP) in 1987. The NCTHP is an effort to systematically collect and preserve the history of Nye County. The centerpiece of the NCTHP is a large set of interviews conducted with individuals who had knowledge of local history. The interviews provide a composite view of community and county history, revealing the flow of life and events for a part of Nevada that has heretofore been largely neglected by historians. Each interview was recorded, transcribed, and then edited lightly to preserve the language and speech patterns of those interviewed. All oral history interviews have been printed on acid-free paper and bound and archived in Nye County libraries, Special Collections in the James R. Dickinson Library at the University of Nevada, Las Vegas, and at other archival sites located throughout Nevada.

Collection of the oral histories has been accompanied by the assembling of a set of photographs depicting each community's history. These pictures have been obtained from participants in the oral history interviews and other present and past Nye County residents. Complete sets of these photographs have been archived along with the oral histories.

The oral histories and photo collections, as well as written sources, served as the basis for the preparation of this volume on Beatty history. It is one of a series on the history of all major Nye County communities.

In a real sense this volume, like the others in the NCTHP series, is the result of a community effort. Before the oral interviews were conducted, a number of local residents provided advice on which community members had lived in the area the longest, possessed and recalled information not available to others, and were available and willing to participate. Because of time and budgetary constraints, many highly qualified persons were not interviewed.

Following the interviews, the participants gave even more of their time and energy: They elaborated upon and clarified points made during the taped interviews; they went through family albums and identified photographs; and they located books, dates, family records, and so forth. During the preparation of this manuscript, a number of community members were contacted, sometimes repeatedly (if asked, some would probably readily admit that they felt pestered), to answer questions that arose during the writing and editing of the manuscript. Moreover, once the manuscript was in more or less final form, each individual who was discussed for more than a paragraph or two in the text was provided with a copy of his or her portion of the text and was asked to check that portion for errors. Appropriate changes were then made.

Once that stage was completed, several individuals in the Beatty area were asked to review the entire manuscript for errors of omission and commission. At each stage, this quality-control process resulted in the elimination of factual errors and raised our confidence in the validity of the contents.

The author's training as an anthropologist, not a historian (although the difference between the disciplines is often probably less than some might suppose), likely has something to do with the community approach taken in the preparation of this volume. It also may contribute to the focus on the details of individuals and their families as opposed to a description of residents and their communities. Perhaps this volume, as well as a concern with variability among individuals and their contribution to a community, reflects an "ethnographic," as opposed to a "historical," perspective on local history. In the author's view, there is no such thing as "the history" of a community; there are many histories of a community. A community's history is like a sunrise—the colors are determined by a multitude of factors, such as the time of year, weather, and point of view. This history of Beatty was greatly determined by the input of those who helped produce it. If others had participated, both the subjects treated and the relative emphasis the subjects received would have been, at least, somewhat different.

Many basic facts would, of course, remain much the same—names, dates, and locations of events. But the focus, the details illustrating how facts and human beings come together, would have been different. History is, and always will remain, sensitive to perspective and impressionistic, in the finest and most beautiful sense of the word.

A longer and more thoroughly referenced (though non-illustrated) companion to this volume, titled *A History of Beatty, Nevada*, is also available through Nye County Press. Virtually all written material contained in this volume was obtained from the longer volume. Those who desire more comprehensive referencing should consult the longer version of Beatty's history.

I hope readers enjoy this history of Beatty, Nevada. The town of Beatty began as a small, unpretentious satellite of the glamorous Rhyolite. Rhyolite, the last of Nevada's great boom camps, burst on the turn-of-the-century mining scene like a little supernova; it faded almost as quickly. Rhyolite disappeared so quickly that within a few years all that remained of the city whose population is said to have peaked above 10,000 (Weight, 1972:26) was a handful of intact buildings surrounded by crumbling facades of once-elegant structures, stark reminders of faded hopes. Harold O. and Lucile Weight called their history of Rhyolite (first edition 1953) *Death Valley's Ghost City of Golden Dreams*—an appropriate title for a book about a place that has fascinated so many. There is more than a little of Rhyolite in all of us. It symbolizes the world as we would like it to be—the world of our dreams, the world of our hopes and our imaginations. Rhyolite's dramatic and sudden appearance on the Nye County desert tells us that dreams can come true. Yet there is another message: Rhyolite's equally rapid disappearance tells us to be cautious, not to be deceived—dreams can come true but usually don't. Rhyolite tells us to beware of wishful thinking, promises of con men, and promoters out for a fast buck. In contrast to Rhyolite, Beatty is reality. Though it lacks the glamor of the flash-in-the-pan, Beatty represents honesty, reliability, stability, and steadiness of values and growth. Of all the towns spawned from the Rhyolite boom—Bullfrog, Gold Center, Carrarra, Leadfield, Lee, Rose's Well, Amargosa, Transvaal, Springdale, Pioneer, and many more—Beatty is the only one to survive and grow. Its salubrious climate, ample water, fortuitous location, and friendly citizens assure it will be there for a long time to come.

Robert D. McCracken

Acknowledgments

This volume was produced under the Nye County Town History Project, initiated by the Nye County Board of Commissioners. Appreciation goes to Chairman Joe S. Garcia, Jr., Robert "Bobby" N. Revert, and Pat Mankins; Mr. Revert and Mr. Garcia, in particular, showed deep interest and unyielding support for the project from its inception. Thanks also go to current commissioners Richard L. Carver and Barbara J. Raper, who joined Mr. Revert on the board and who continued the project with enthusiastic support. Commissioners Dave Hannigan, Joe Maslach, and Cameron McRae—all elected in 1990—have provided on-going commitment. Stephen T. Bradhurst, Jr., planning consultant for Nye County, gave unwavering support and advocacy, provided advice and input regarding the conduct of the research, and constantly served as a sounding board as production problems were worked out. This volume would never have been possible without the enthusiastic support of the Nye County commissioners and Mr. Bradhurst.

Thanks go to the participants of the Nye County Town History Project, especially those from the Beatty area, who kindly provided much of the information; thanks, also, to residents from Beatty and throughout southern Nevada—too numerous to mention by name—who provided assistance and historical information.

Jean Charney, Jean Stoess, and Sandra Rush did the word processing and, along with Gary Roberts, Maire Hayes, and Jodie Hansen, provided editorial comments, review, and suggestions. Alice Levine and Michelle Starika edited several drafts of the manuscript and contributed measurably to this volume's scholarship and readability. Alice Levine also served as production consultant. Polly Christensen was responsible for re-design and layout. Gretchen Loeffler and Bambi McCracken assisted in numerous secretarial and clerical duties.

Jack Crowell, Maud-Kathrin Crowell, Ralph Lisle, Chloe Lisle, Art Revert, and Robert N. Revert kindly critiqued several drafts of the manuscript, made many thoughtful comments, and graciously answered many questions. Dave Hannigan, William J. Metscher, and Deborah A. Stetz reviewed the final draft and made useful comments. Kevin Rafferty and Lynda Blair, from the University of Nevada, Las Vegas, Environmental Research Center, provided helpful suggestions on the section concerning the archaeology of Native Americans in the Beatty area. Phillip Earl of the Nevada Historical Society contributed valuable support and criticism throughout, and helped obtain several rare photographs reproduced in this volume. Shirley Harding, museum curator, Death Valley National Monument, also assisted in securing a number of photos from the museum's collection. Tom King at the Oral History Program of the University of Nevada, Reno, served as consulting oral historian. Susan Jarvis, Kathy War, and Dennis McBride of Special Collections, James R. Dickinson Library, University of Nevada, Las Vegas, assisted greatly with research conducted at that institution. Much deserved thanks are extended to all these persons.

All aspects of production of this volume were supported by the U.S. Department of Energy, Grant No. DE-FG08-89NV10820. However, any opinions, findings, conclusions, or recommendations expressed herein are those of the author and do not necessarily reflect the views of DOE. Any errors or deficiencies are, of course, the author's responsibility.

R. D. M.

Beatty:

Frontier Oasis

Map of southern Nye County, Nevada (1881), showing the relative undeveloped character of the Beatty–Amargosa Valley area. Twenty-three years later, in 1904, the town of Beatty would be located approximately where the "G" in "Great Amargosa Desert" is printed on the west side of the Bare Mountains. Nye County Town History Project—Slavin Collection

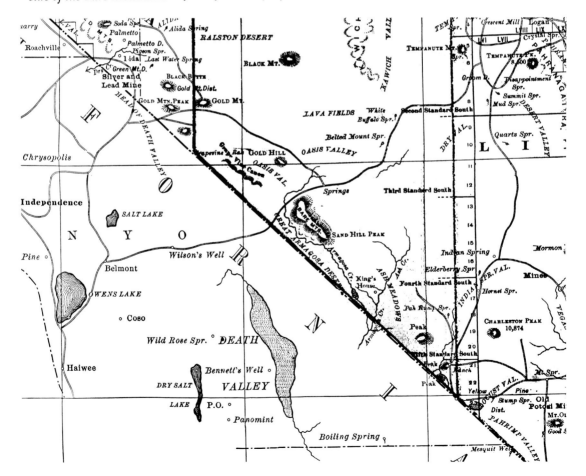

CHAPTER ONE

The Land and Early Inhabitants

The great booms in Tonopah, Goldfield, and Rhyolite represent the last major flowering of the Old West in the United States. The chance discoveries of large deposits of gold and silver; the rush to claim a share of the new wealth; the explosive and often chaotic growth of rowdy boomtowns—usually followed by their equally rapid decline; the influx of serious promoters and flashy flimflam men; the arrival of merchants, teamsters, camp followers, schoolteachers, wives, and children; the growth of farms and ranches to feed the new towns; the hope of good luck and quick riches; and the deeply held values of personal freedom, independence, hard work, and a capacity to tolerate the extremes of nature— these were all part of the final mining boom episode.

Of all the towns spawned by the Rhyolite boom, the community of Beatty, Nevada, is the only one that survived. The others have vanished; the only evidence they existed are a few fading trails, deteriorating building foundations, an occasional stone facade of a bank or hotel, and scattered solitary mine dumps beside mute holes in the hills.

Location, Terrain, and Surrounding Features

Beatty, Nevada, is located in southern Nye County, about 12 miles east of Nevada's diagonal border with California. It is situated on the southeastern margin of the Bullfrog Hills, a range of mountains of relatively modest height. The highest point in the Bullfrog Hills, which would be called mountains anywhere else, is Sawtooth Mountain, which rises to an elevation of 6002 feet.

The Amargosa River, once described as a "feeble trickle," is the only stream of drinkable water within a radius of 40 miles. It originates from springs about 10 miles north of Beatty at Springdale and flows south down Oasis Valley through Beatty. It passes through the Beatty Narrows, located about 1 mile south of town, and enters the Amargosa Valley where it immediately sinks into underground channels. Then it flows southeastward down the Amargosa Valley, crosses the Nevada-California border, eventually turning northwest, to become lost in Death Valley.

The Funeral and the Grapevine mountains, which form the eastern margin of Death Valley and the western margin of Amargosa Valley and Sarcobatus Flat, respectively, lie about 10 miles west of Beatty and are crossed at Daylight Pass (probably originally called Delight Pass) by Highway 374. The old mining camp of Chloride Cliff is about 5 miles southeast of the Daylight Pass summit. Highway 267 crosses the Grapevine Mountains at Grapevine Canyon where Death Valley Scotty's Castle is located and then enters the northern end of Death Valley.

The majority of the principal mining communities in the Beatty area during its frontier boom period were located either in or on the margin of the Bullfrog Hills and include, in addition to Beatty, Rhyolite (4 miles west of Beatty), Bullfrog (1 mile south of Rhyolite), Gold Center (just south of the Beatty Narrows), and Pioneer (5 miles north of Beatty). All except Beatty are now ghost towns.

The nearest modern settlement to Beatty is Amargosa Valley, a small community with a relatively dispersed population, located primarily south of U.S. Highway 95 in the Amargosa Valley about 25 miles to the south; Las Vegas is 120 miles to the southeast. Goldfield is located about 65 miles north of Beatty on Highway 95; Tonopah is about 90 miles to the north. Furnace Creek, situated in the heart of Death Valley, is about 40 miles south of Beatty. Immediately east and north of Beatty lie the Nevada Test Site and the Nellis Air Force Range, the huge federal facility that occupies a large part of southern Nevada and is off limits to the public.

Early Residents of the Beatty Area

Archaeological evidence in Beatty and Oasis Valley is sparse; few sites that might provide significant information about early inhabitants have been found. It is not possible to precisely state when human beings first entered the Beatty area. It seems likely that a culture of hunters and gatherers, known as the Clovis people, inhabited the area by 11,000 years ago. The Clovis culture is believed to have been based primarily on hunting, focusing on a number of species of large, now extinct, mammals, including the mammoth, camel, and giant sloth.

The first people to live in the Beatty area about whom we have more than scant information are the Western Shoshone who lived in the unusually harsh and barren environment; in some places the land was more barren than portions of Death Valley because the mountain ranges in the territory of the Beatty Indians were not as high as those in some adjoining areas and thus there was less moisture. It is estimated that in the latter half of the nineteenth century, the Indians in Beatty had a lower population density per square mile than most other Indian groups of the Great Basin.

Native Americans (probably Shoshone or Southern Paiute), Rhyolite, circa 1906. Note the use of blankets to keep warm and the building constructed of rough-sawed lumber and canvas.

Nevada Historical Society

Native Americans (probably Shoshone) in the Beatty-Rhyolite area, 1907. Nevada Historical Society

Reproduction of a postcard featuring Aurora, a Shoshone Indian resident of Beatty, circa 1937. Aurora was well known for her basket-making skills. Nye County Town History Project—Reidhead Collection

Prior to the arrival of Europeans, the Western Shoshone practiced a hunting and gathering way of life. They lived as seminomads, moving within a defined geographical area where wild plants and game were available. Each family was, in all but a few activities, a self-sufficient economic unit. Tasks within each small group were divided according to gender. Women usually prepared the food, did the housekeeping, fashioned baskets and pottery, and made most of the family's clothing. They also collected seeds and other plant foods, although the men helped in collecting pine nuts. Men hunted, made stone tools, weapons, digging sticks, and rabbit-skin blankets, and built their dwellings—conical-shaped huts consisting of a light frame covered with bark for winter use and a semicircular sunshade for summer.

In about 1875, there were six camps of Shoshone Indians in the immediate vicinity of Beatty; the camps were located along the Amargosa River in Oasis Valley and in the flat at the present site of Beatty. There were a total of 29 persons in four of these camps, and the other two camps were alternate sites. Numerous temporary camps were located at other watered sites in this area, which consisted of about 1300 square miles.

Beginning in the second half of the nineteenth century, incursions of Europeans and others into their territory began to disrupt the traditional way of life of the Western Shoshone in the Beatty area. The loss of or damage to many traditional plant collection sites; reduction in game, garden areas, and camp sites; and the decimation of the already small population due to European diseases took their toll. Rather than live apart from the strangers who often occupied the most productive parts of their land, the Indians who did not perish from disease congregated around the settlements that sprang up in the area; they worked as laborers, ranch hands, and domestics. From the 1920s through the 1940s, a few ramshackle Indian dwellings were located in Beatty across the railroad tracks on both sides of the Amargosa River. After the 1940s, the residents dispersed to reservations at Walker Lake, Reese River, Duckwater, and other areas or were absorbed into Beatty itself.

Old Man Beatty's Ranch, Beatty, 1906. Montillus (Montillion) Murray "Old Man" Beatty (after whom the town of Beatty is named) is in the background; his three children are in the foreground. Beatty's Ranch is located on the east side of Highway 95 just north of the present (1991) limits of the community. National Park Service—Death Valley National Monument

CHAPTER TWO

Exploration and Settlement

Due to the inhospitable character of the region, the Beatty area was usually bypassed by the early explorers of the American West. Typically, early explorers followed seacoasts and lakefronts, rivers, and Indian trails when entering a new area. Attracted to verdant valleys and well-watered mountain ranges, which offered potential for abundance of wild game (especially beaver), they tended to follow naturally existing transportation corridors that minimized distances and were more likely to provide water, food for them and their animals, and shelter. The great barren region that was made of rugged mountain ranges, separated by dry desert valleys stretching for 100 or more miles in any direction from Beatty, offered none of these advantages.

Expeditions of Odgen and Fremont

It is possible that the famous Canadian explorer-trapper, Peter Skene Ogden, passed through the area where Beatty is now located on his 1829–1830 Snake Country Expedition, which originated in the Columbia River region, moved south to the Humboldt River in northern Nevada, and eventually "followed the eastern foothills of the Sierra southward to Walker Lake" (Cline, 1974:91). After leaving Walker Lake, Ogden passed through some highly inhospitable country, "traveling parallel to what is now the boundary between California and Nevada," perhaps passing through what is now the Nellis Air Force Range. On that passage, Ogden and his men experienced great hardships; they suffered from cold and hunger and went days without water. Their horses became weak and some died; the men were reduced to satisfying their hunger on the horses' carcasses and quenching their thirst on their blood. Ogden's expedition eventually ended at the Gulf of California; he may have traveled through the Beatty area, perhaps moving south down the Oasis Valley.

Colonel John C. Fremont in 1850 at age 37. Though Fremont never saw the site of the town of Beatty, he led a number of expeditions into the vast, little-explored region known as the Great Basin; on his fifth and last expedition, Fremont passed north of the Beatty area on his way to California. University of Nevada, Las Vegas—Dickinson Library Special Collections

On his fifth and last expedition (1853–1854), Colonel John C. Fremont passed to the north of the Beatty area on his way to California. Fremont, who was looking for a suitable railroad route across the southwest, left Cedar City, Utah, in late February 1854 and struck out across the unexplored Escalante Desert. Fremont's party had had a difficult time in Utah, attempting to cross some of the most rugged country in the American West in the middle of one of the coldest winters the Mormons had experienced in their decade there. The group "entered Nevada south of present-day Pioche and kept moving [passing north of Beatty] through a series of snowstorms until [it] reached the granite barrier of the Sierra Nevada at the thirty-seventh parallel, a little south of present-day Bishop, California" (Egan, 1985:503).

Early Settlers

The Oasis Valley and the Beatty vicinity remained isolated and unsettled by whites until the 1870s. The development of a few mines in the area eventually resulted in the establishment of some small ranching operations.

Eugene Lander, a prospector from San Bernardino, is usually credited with being the first white settler in the Beatty area. He was hard-working and industrious but never lucky; at least twice he was fairly close to the big bonanza, but he never struck it rich. Lander had two prospecting partners—August J. Franklin and a man named Hanson. High in the Funeral Mountains near Daylight Pass on the morning of August 13, 1871, Franklin spotted some promising float while he was killing a rattlesnake. The next day, he and Hanson followed the float to its source on the crest of the range and found a great quartz belt laced with what they thought was silver chloride. Rough assays done in San Bernardino indicated the rock ran from $200 to $1000 a ton in silver. The three brought in friends as partners in the claim and formed the Chloride Cliff Mining Company. Soon they found that what they thought was silver chloride was really lead chloride, worth less than $28 a ton.

Lander quit the Chloride Cliff Mine but continued to prospect in the hills surrounding the upper Amargosa for nearly a decade. About 15 miles northeast of Chloride Cliff, across the Amargosa Valley on Bare Mountain (about 5 miles east and a little south of present-day Beatty), he found a large ledge of "black metal" in November 1879. He called it the Blue Monster in an area he named the Bromide mining district.

While Lander worked the pockety ores of the Blue Monster, he started a small ranch in 1879 in Oasis Valley, just north of the present site of Beatty. He stayed for a few years; when he moved on, his old partner William M. Stockton acquired the ranch September 22, 1882. In 1886, Thomas W. Brooks, a southern California resident, traveled from Los Angeles to Oasis Valley and wrote a series of newspaper articles about his journey. Brooks wrote of his arrival at Stockton's ranch in Oasis Valley and gives us a wonderful, detailed description of the terrain around the ranch.

> Mr. Stockton's ranch is situated two miles above the mouth of the canyon, on the northern border of the plains which we had just crossed, and in the lower southern end of the Oasis or upper valley of the Amargosa River, Nye County, Nevada. It is properly called Oasis (a fertile spot surrounded by barren waste or desert); innumerable springs of cold and hot water; a rich soil which will produce in large quantities any of the varieties of field or garden produce; and a never-failing meadow, densely covered with a good quality of grass (Brooks, 1970: 20).

By 1890 George Lynch, George Davis and his family, John Howell, Jack Longstreet, and Montillus "Old Man" Beatty had also settled in Oasis Valley. Not much is known about Lynch and Davis except that Lynch was not "at home" very much (Ritter, 1939 [1982]:1). In 1895 John Howell, the first known black resident of the Beatty area, tried his luck at ranching in Oasis Valley.

Andrew Jackson "Jack" Longstreet, a long-term resident of Nye County and legendary desert frontiersman, owned a ranch in the Moapa Valley and by 1890 had taken up a 160-acre homestead in the upper end of Oasis Valley. At that time he was one of three white men living in a 7000-square-mile area.

"Old Man" Beatty (Montillus [Montillion] Murray Beatty), for whom Beatty is named, was a native of Iowa; he enlisted in the Union Army at Lyons, Iowa, on May 6, 1861, and served in Company I, Second Iowa Infantry Regiment. He was discharged because of disability and came west after the Civil War. Beatty, who

Few photos of Old Man Beatty are known to exist. This photo, reprinted in many sources, seems to have been a clipping from an old newspaper or book. Nye County Town History Project—Lisle Collection

Beatty's Ranch, located just north of Beatty, perhaps around 1920 or earlier. Beatty sold the ranch in 1906. Nye County Town History Project—Lemmon Collection

said he crossed Death Valley every month of the year, worked as a miner at Gold Mountain and in the Amargosa Valley. He acquired the Lander Ranch in spring 1896, not long after William Stockton's death. Beatty married a full-blooded Paiute woman and they had at least three children, Maud, Frank, and Monte. He was described as a "generous, hardworking family man who made his ranch a welcome home to all who passed that way" (Lingenfelter, 1986:168).

He was Beatty's first postmaster when the post office opened January 19, 1905, although he could neither read nor write, except for his name. Beatty sold his ranch and its springs in 1906 to the Bullfrog Water, Power, and Light Company for $10,000 and began a new ranch at Cow Creek in Death Valley. He continued to dabble in mining until his death in December 1908. Mrs. Beatty died in Beatty in February 1910.

The Beatty Area at the Turn of the Century

In the early 1900s, the area was still very much frontier. "Old Man" Beatty and his family occupied the stone house on his place at the lower end of Oasis Valley and John Howell was farther up the valley. To the south there were a few settlers at Ash Meadows, with a couple of large ranches and a handful of smaller operations in both the Pahrump and Las Vegas valleys. There was a ranch at Indian Springs. More than 150 miles to the northeast as the crow flies, the mining town of Pioche, founded in the late 1860s, was past its prime as was Hiko, 100 miles from Beatty, at the north end of the Pahranagat Valley. A few ranchers were well established in the Pahranagat Valley. The first community east of Beatty that was more than a bar, a post office, and a one-room schoolhouse was Delamar, which was 50 miles south of Pioche. Belmont, 125 miles north of Beatty, was also past its prime, and Tonopah's silver and Goldfield's gold had not yet been discovered. Gold had been found in the hills separating the Amargosa and Pahrump valleys in the 1890s and there were several gold camps in the Panamints, the most important of which was Ballarat, named after the famous Australian gold rush camp of the 1850s.

In late 1904 and early 1905, numerous small mines dotted the surrounding hills of the Rhyolite area. This photo shows the Gold Bar Mine, near Bullfrog, Nevada, probably early 1905. Central Nevada Historical Society

CHAPTER THREE

The Boom Is On

The gold in the green rock at Bullfrog had been there for millions of years, but it took the keen eye of an individual who could recognize what he saw to make the discovery. God put the gold at Bullfrog, but it wasn't for anybody to find. It took someone who knew about different types of rocks and the geologic formations and the indications of where gold might occur. It took someone who could survive on the desert with a burro, a blanket, and a gold pan, and who could travel 30 miles on foot between water holes. It took someone who knew loneliness, a man of the desert, a true pioneer, a starry-eyed dreamer, a chaser of rainbows, perhaps even a fool, a ne'er-do-well by some standards—a prospector.

The Montgomery Brothers: The Boom Begins

The Montgomery brothers, George, Frank, and Ernest Alexander (also known as Bob), started the great gold boom in the Death Valley area. They found the gold that opened the rush, they were behind the opening of the first big mines, and they stayed for more than twenty years until the boom was over. The Montgomery brothers were born in Canada and moved with their parents to a farm in Stuart, Iowa, after the Civil War. In 1884 they went west and worked in the mines in Wood River, Idaho. George, who arrived in 1890, was the first of the brothers to come to Death Valley; while looking for the Lost Breyfogle Mine, he discovered the Chispa Mine (*chispa* is Spanish for "nugget") about 50 miles southeast of the Bullfrog Hills in the Last Chance Range, which separates the Amargosa and Pahrump valleys. The discovery was one of several in the area. A few months later, about 4 miles to the north, the deposit at Johnnie was found by John Tecopa, the son of Chief Tecopa; and the Younts discovered the North Belle Mine a short distance away at about the same time.

TONOPAH **INDIAN SPRINGS** LAS VEGAS
MILES ELEVATION, 3120 FT 43 MILES

Ernest Alexander "Bob" Montgomery (fourth from the left, wearing suspenders) with unidentified men at what is likely the Las Vegas and Tonopah Railroad depot, Indian Springs, Nevada, 1915. Montgomery, who lived to be 91, would have been about 51 when this picture was taken. Nevada Historical Society

Bob Montgomery prospecting somewhere in southern Nevada, perhaps in the Indian Springs area, 1915.

Nevada Historical Society

In 1896 the Montgomery brothers discovered gold in the Panamint Mountains and named their claim the World Beater Mine. Eventually, the town of Ballarat was established nearby. In 1897 Bob Montgomery and a couple of partners made yet another discovery in a nearby canyon and named it for their favorite whiskey: Oh Be Joyful. By 1900 Ballarat was the leading camp in the Panamints, with nearly 300 men working in the area mines. But the discoveries at Tonopah in 1900 led to a mass exodus from the Panamints and Ballarat in 1901, and most of what was left of the town was destroyed by a flash flood that summer. In 1903 George Montgomery returned to Ballarat to restake his claim on the abandoned World Beater, which produced significant quantities of bullion before the high grade was exhausted in 1905. In 1905 discoveries at Bullfrog once again led to abandonment of Ballarat. Bob Montgomery had left Ballarat and settled in Tonopah in 1901. He married and began to work as a jeweler and an optician, but his passion for gold was only temporarily cooled.

Shorty Harris and Ed Cross: "Lousy with Gold"

Frank "Shorty" Harris and Ernest "Ed" Cross are credited with the discovery on August 4, 1904, of "the fabulous gold-speckled green rock" found in the Bullfrog Hills a few miles southwest of what was to become the town of Rhyolite (Weight, 1972:3). Born in Rhode Island on July 21, 1857, Harris was orphaned at the age of seven. In the late 1870s he rode the rails west to seek his fortune in the mines. He searched in Leadville, Tombstone, the Coeur d'Alenes, and Death Valley. Harris, called Short Man by the local Indians, had a big, bushy mustache, blue eyes, big ears, and was barely 5'4" tall. He was known for his weakness for whiskey—the Oh Be Joyful. Cross has been described as a quiet, sober young newlywed (Lingenfelter, 1986:203). Shorty and Ed always disagreed about who really made the Bullfrog discovery. According to Shorty,

> I didn't get in early enough at Tonopah and Goldfield, so I wandered south and followed the Keane Wonder excitement in the Funeral range. I got there about as late as I did elsewhere, so I didn't get any close-in ground. Long before the Keane Wonder was struck, I had traveled across the country from Grapevine to Buck Springs, and had seen the big blowout of quartz and quartzite on the ground that later I located as the Bullfrog claim. When I found that I couldn't get anything good at the Keane Wonder, I remembered the blowout and decided to go back to it. E. L. Cross was at the Keane Wonder; he was there afoot.
> "Shorty, I'd like to go with you," said Cross.
> "Your chance is good," said I. "Come along!" (Ritter, 1939 [1982]:1–2).

In a 1930 interview for *Westways*, Shorty Harris described what next happened:

> So we left the Keane Wonder, went through Boundary Canyon, and made camp at Buck Springs, five miles from a ranch on the Amargosa where a squaw man by the name of Monte Beatty lived. The next morning while Ed was cooking, I went after the burros. They were feeding on the side of a mountain near our camp, and about half a mile from the spring. I carried my pick, as all prospectors do, even when they are looking for their jacks—a man never knows just when he is going to locate pay-ore. When I reached the burros, they were right on the spot where the

Quintessential desert prospector Shorty Harris, co-discoverer of the deposit of gold in the green rock at Bullfrog, Nevada, as he appeared some years after the lucky find. University of Nevada, Las Vegas—Dickinson Library Special Collections

Ernest "Ed" Cross, dressed in miner's garb, at an unknown location years after he and Shorty discovered gold at Bullfrog. Nevada Historical Society

Bullfrog mine was afterwards located. Two hundred feet away was a ledge of rock with some copper stains on it. I walked over and broke off a piece with my pick— and gosh, I couldn't believe my own eyes. The chunks of gold were so big that I could see them at arm's length—regular jewelry stone! In fact, a lot of that ore was sent to jewelers in this country and England, and they set it in rings, it was that pretty! Right then, it seemed to me that the whole mountain was gold.

I let out a yell, and Ed knew something had happened; so he came running up as fast as he could. When he got close enough to hear, I yelled again:

"Ed, we've got the world by the tail, or else we're coppered!"

We broke off several more pieces, and they were like the first—just lousy with gold. The rock was green, almost like turquoise, spotted with big chunks of yellow metal, and looked a lot like the back of a frog. This gave us an idea for naming our claim, so we called it the Bullfrog. The formation had a good dip, too. It looked like a real fissure vein; the kind that goes deep and has lots of real stuff in it. We hunted over that mountain for more outcroppings, but there were no others like the one the burros led me to. We had tumbled into the cream pitcher on the first one—so why waste time looking for skimmed milk?

That night we built a hot fire with greasewood, and melted the gold out of the specimens. We wanted to see how much was copper, and how much was the real stuff. And when the pan got red hot, and that gold ran out and formed a button, we knew that our strike was a big one, and that we were rich (Harris, 1930:18).

According to Shorty, the two waited until the next day to locate claims. Then they went over and showed the rich rock to Old Man Beatty, who immediately rushed over and located his own claim. George Davis heard about the strike and staked some ground for himself to the east. Harris and Cross told M. M. Detch, Len McGarry, and Bob Montgomery—the word quickly spread and the great Rhyolite boom was on.

In his version, Cross said he made the valuable discovery. In a 1946 interview, he gave the following account:

One morning while digging and sampling, I picked up a specimen about the size of a hen's egg. It gave me a little shiver of excitement and I could tell by the feel of it that it ran heavy with gold. It lay on the surface, in fact the glisten of it in the sunlight was what drew my attention to it. When I was sure my first impression was correct, I called Shorty. With a skeptical smile Shorty looked at it, hefted it, then began the usual tests. Watching him as he worked, I saw his cheeks change color. There was excitement in his eyes, and his fingers trembled. Suddenly he let out a warwhoop, jumped, and shouted, "Hell-fire, Eddie, we've struck the richest jackpot this side of the Klondike! Let's get busy as pack-rats and stake our claims!" (Murray, 1963:8)

The Bullfrog Mine (probably 1905), the site of Shorty and Ed's original discovery.
Central Nevada Historical Society

Montgomery "Re-infected" with Gold Fever

Bob Montgomery heard about the discovery at Bullfrog from Shorty Harris and Ed Cross when the two prospectors were in Goldfield. In September 1904, Montgomery headed for Bullfrog on a $75 grubstake by three Goldfield investors. He was unsuccessful and stayed only a few days. On the way back to Goldfield, he stopped at John Howell's ranch in Oasis Valley. There he met a young Shoshone known as Hungry Johnny, who claimed to know where ore could be found. Montgomery hired him to stake out two claims. Three weeks later, they met at Old Man Beatty's ranch and Hungry Johnny showed Montgomery the claims.

The claims, seemingly only a crumbly deposit of pink talc, did not look promising, but Montgomery took a chance and staked out two more adjoining claims—the Shoshone Nos. 2 and 3. The first assays ran less than $5 per ton. Montgomery took more samples and was still having no luck when, for an interest in the claims, a wizened old prospector named Al James agreed to show Montgomery where good gold values could be obtained on the Shoshone No. 3. Montgomery took samples in the talc where James designated and they ran $300 per ton in gold. An experienced miner, Montgomery wanted to get under the ore and cut it at depth and so a tunnel was driven below the deposit. He struck ore 70 feet thick that was assayed as high as $16,000 a ton. Tears filled Bob Montgomery's eyes when he first saw his new bonanza: "I have struck it; the thing that I have dreamed about since I was 15 years old has come true; I am fixed for life and nobody can take it away from me," he said. His find was heralded as "the greatest discovery ever made on the desert," "richer than the mines of King Solomon" (Lingenfelter, 1986:208). Montgomery's discovery and reports of fabulous assays from surrounding claims were ballyhooed nationwide.

Shorty Loses His Claim and Rhyolite Booms

After Harris and Cross made their discovery, they had assays run in Goldfield. The first showed $665 a ton in gold, and other samples reached $3000. Once in Goldfield, Shorty characteristically headed for the saloons and the Oh Be Joyful. Cross quickly lined up a sale of their claims for $10,000, but the deal could not be completed because Shorty could not be found to close it. Shorty sobered up six days later, only to find that while he was in a drunken stupor he had sold his half of the claim for the low price of $1000, which he promptly spent on more drinks.

Shorty Harris and Ed Cross were in Goldfield for only a few days. But word of their discovery in the Bullfrog Hills spread quickly. Goldfield and Tonopah were filled with "boomers," who had gotten to those towns too late to stake a valuable claim or in some other way to capitalize on the excitement. Most did not wait around for Shorty and Ed to head south to their claims; they gathered what information they could on the location and struck out on their own. Time was of the essence; a delay of a few hours, even a few minutes, could mean the difference between becoming rich and getting nothing.

> When Ed and I got back to our claim [Shorty speaks of the claim as his, but he had sold his interest] a week later, more than a thousand men were camped around it,

Bullfrog, Nevada, November 1905. The growth of nearby Rhyolite drew population away from the smaller towns that had sprung up in the vicinity, including Bullfrog. The community of Bullfrog was rapidly eclipsed by the booming Rhyolite and on May 4, 1906, the Rhyolite Herald *bragged, "verily, the BULLFROG CROAKETH" (Weight, 1972:12).* Central Nevada Historical Society—Nevada Historical Society Collection

Bullfrog, Nevada, 1905. Persons unidentified. Central Nevada Historical Society—Nevada Historical Society Collection

Bakery, Bullfrog, Nevada, 1905. Persons unidentified. Central Nevada Historical Society—Nevada Historical Society Collection

and they were coming in every day. A few had tents, but most of 'em were in open camps. One man had brought a wagonload of whiskey, pitched a tent, and made a bar by laying a plank across two barrels. He was serving the liquor in tincups, and doing a fine business.

That was the start of Rhyolite, and from then on things moved so fast that it made even us oldtimers dizzy. Men were swarming all over the mountains like ants, staking out claims, digging and blasting, and hurrying back to the county seat to record their holdings. There were extensions on all sides of our claim, and other claims covering the country in all directions.

In a few days, wagonloads of lumber began to arrive, and the first buildings were put up. These were called rag-houses because they were half boards and half canvas. But this building material was so expensive that lots of men made dugouts, which didn't cost much more than plenty of sweat and blisters (Harris, 1930:19).

By September 1904, there were 75 men camped at Beatty's ranch alone. A returning Goldfielder met 52 outfits headed toward the new bonanza. "'What a procession!' the *Rhyolite Herald* recalled. 'Men on foot, burros, mule teams, freights, light rigs, saddle outfits, automobiles, houses on wheels—all coming down the line from Tonopah and Goldfield, raising a string of dust 100 miles long'" (Weight, 1972:7).

A covey of towns sprang up in the area adjoining the big strike. By mid-March 1905, Bullfrog had 20 tents and a population of 40; Amargosa, located 1 mile below Bullfrog, had 80 tents and a population of 160; Rhyolite had 100 tents and a population of 200; Bonanza had 1 tent; Gold Center had 20 tents; and the town of Beatty, the most propitiously located of all the communities in terms of the availability of water, had 150 tents and a population of 300. Rhyolite, which lay

Rhyolite, Nevada, probably 1905 or early 1906. The community was still primarily a tent town. Central Nevada Historical Society

Desert prospecting outfit belonging to the Smith Brothers operating out of Beatty, 1906. This outfit was considered one of the best equipped in the area. National Park Service—Death Valley National Monument

Opening of Rhyolite's first permanent school, January 29, 1906. At the end of April 1907, the teacher, E. Louise Presser, was forced to take a vacation in order to avoid suffering a nervous breakdown brought on by the stress of teaching too many pupils in the small building. The school, which was financed by donations and basket socials, was soon replaced by a two-story structure costing $20,000. Beatty, Nevada, Library

in a horseshoe-shaped valley at the base of the mountains below Montgomery's Shoshone Mine, became the center of activity for the district; and the Shoshone became the "boss mine" of the Bullfrog district (Lingenfelter, 1986:209).

With characteristic hyperbole, Harris described Rhyolite's growth:

Rhyolite grew like a mushroom. Gold Center was started four miles away, and Beatty's ranch became a town within a few months. There were 12,000 people in the three places, and two railroads were built out to Rhyolite. Shipments of gold were made every day, and some of the ore was so rich that it was sent by express with armed guards. And then a lot of cash came into Rhyolite—more than went out from the mines. It was this sucker money that put the town on the map quick. The stock exchange was doing a big business, and I remember that the price of Montgomery-Shoshone got up to ten dollars a share (Harris, 1930:19–20).

Senator William M. Stewart, a Comstock veteran and a renowned Nevada politician and mining lawyer, became a resident of Bullfrog. Senator Stewart owned an entire block on Main Street in Bullfrog, and his office and residence were the finest in the district. His office included a 1200-volume law library, said to be the best in the state (with the possible exception of the State Library at Carson City). Stewart is quoted as saying, "If I had twenty grandsons I would plant them all in Bullfrog and let them grow up to be millionaires during the course of this present decade. . . . I look forward to seeing the early days of Cripple Creek and

The Overbury Building, named for John T. Overbury, was located on Golden Street. It was one of the finest structures in Rhyolite. The stone from which the building was constructed was said to have run from $4 to $10 a ton in gold. The building featured modern plumbing, electric wiring, and had a fire plug and fire hose on every floor, with a 5,000-gallon water tank on the roof for emergencies. Central Nevada Historical Society Collection

Goldfield duplicated." From the district, he said, "would arise in time the greatest camp the West has ever seen" (Weight, 1972:10).

But eventually Bullfrog faded and by the end of May 1905, its population of 300 was eclipsed by Rhyolite's 1500. There were 20 saloons operating in Rhyolite then. Initially, water was unavailable in Rhyolite and had to be hauled from Beatty by burro in whiskey barrels. The water tasted like whiskey and sold for $5 a barrel. In the summer of 1905, three rival companies completed pipelines from Beatty, Indian Springs, and Terry Springs to Rhyolite. Telephone service reached Rhyolite early in 1905. Electric power was first generated locally, then brought in from hydroelectric plants on Bishop Creek in California.

By 1907, the population of Rhyolite was 6000, making it the fourth largest town in Nevada, after Goldfield (estimated 20,000), Tonopah (estimated 10,000), and Reno (estimated 8000). In 1907, 50 cars of freight were arriving daily on the Las Vegas and Tonopah Railroad. Lots in the heart of Rhyolite sold for $10,000. In January 1908, the John S. Cook & Co. Bank Building on Golden Street in Rhyolite was completed. The three-story building cost more than $90,000 and was constructed of concrete, steel, and glass, with Italian marble stairs, imported stained glass windows, and Honduran mahogany trim.

The boom, of course, was predicated upon the assumption that the hills around Rhyolite held valuable deposits of gold. The gold would be extracted by mining companies and there was the expectation of high profits, which would be reflected in stock prices. Such excitement led to the formation of more than 200 Bullfrog mining companies, which floated over 200 million shares of stock on the

A burro race, Rhyolite, July 4, 1908. The children of Rhyolite used burros, the ubiquitous nonhuman occupants of desert mining camps, in races. Central Nevada Historical Society—Nevada Historical Society Collection

Camp located at the Gold Bar Mine, near Bullfrog, probably early 1905.
Central Nevada Historical Society

Gold Bar Mill and Mine, January 1908.   Central Nevada Historical Society

public. Most companies incorporated the name Bullfrog: Giant Bullfrog, Bullfrog Merger, Bullfrog Apex, Bullfrog Annex, Bullfrog Gold Dollar, Bullfrog Daisy, Bullfrog Starlight, Bullfrog Puritan, Bullfrog Outlaw, Bullfrog Mogul. Bob Montgomery and his partners formed a stock company, the Montgomery Shoshone Mine Company, in April 1905. Montgomery, who held three-quarters of the stock, boasted that he could take out $10,000 a day from his mine; the first shipment of ore was rumored to average $2300 a ton. There was talk of a big stamp mill to be constructed in Beatty, with a 3-mile aerial tram to the mine, but Montgomery's partners were already seeking a buyer. John W. Brock, the Philadelphia financier who had bought Jim Butler's mine in Tonopah, was approached, but his advisers cautioned him against the purchase because they thought the deposit was superficial.

In early 1906, Bob Montgomery sold his interest in the Montgomery Shoshone Mine to Charles Schwab, "the new saint of the American Dream of rags to riches, the epitome of upward mobility" (Lingenfelter, 1986:217). Schwab had risen from an engineer's helper at the age of eighteen to president and part owner of the Carnegie Steel Company at age thirty-five. Later, Schwab became president of U.S. Steel and was reportedly "the highest salaried man in the world," making over $2 million a year, with stock holdings in the tens of millions (Lingenfelter, 1986:216–217). Under Schwab's ownership nearly 2 miles of tunnels and drifts were developed at the Montgomery Shoshone Mine, and a mill that handled 300 tons per day was constructed at the mine, with water supplied by an 11-mile pipeline from Goss Spring. It was the biggest and most modern mill the Death Valley region had ever seen. Schwab arranged the mine's finances so that he

The Montgomery Shoshone Mine and Mill, Rhyolite, about 1908. The mill, the biggest and most modern in the Death Valley area, produced about $1.5 million in bullion, but never paid a dividend to stockholders. Central Nevada Historical Society—William J. Metcher Collection

would be paid back before any of the stockholders. Such an arrangement proved to be good foresight, for the mine's ore reserves proved to be neither deep nor extensive—the Montgomery Shoshone Mine was closed March 14, 1911. "The Montgomery Shoshone is dead," the March 25 issue of the *Rhyolite Herald* cried. Although the mine had produced $1,418,636.21 in bullion, it never paid a dividend. Its "profit" ($432,000) was partial repayment for Schwab's loans. When the mine closed, the mill and other machinery were sold to pay off the remaining $100,000 he was owed. Shareholder profits, it seemed, had gone "a glimmering" (Lingenfelter, 1986:239).

Although Rhyolite experienced growth from 1904 to about 1907, the boom faded almost as quickly as it had appeared. The ore deposits, apparently lacking size and depth, simply could not long support a boomtown. Deposits might present good indications, but they quickly became exhausted. By disrupting financial markets, the San Francisco earthquake in 1906 slowed development. In reality, the Rhyolite boom was predicated on speculation and could not be sustained. When news of shady dealings involving two of the district's most promising mines surfaced, investor confidence was eroded; and the March 1911 closure of the Montgomery Shoshone, the only mine in the district even to show significant production, was the final blow.

One month later, on April 8, 1911, *Rhyolite Herald* Editor Clemens wrote: "It is with deep regret that I announce my retirement from the newspaper field in the Bullfrog district. It has been my lot to remain here while all my erstwhile contemporaries have fled, one by one, to more inviting localities, and now it is my time to say goodbye" (Weight, 1972:32). Clemens went on to describe Rhyolite as "the prettiest, coziest mining town on the great American desert, a town blessed with ambitious, hopeful, courageous people, and with a climate second to none on earth. Goodbye, dear old Rhyolite." George Probasco, who kept the newspaper going for another month, wrote: "Rhyolite was about the biggest mining boom and bust that ever happened. Until 1908, the sagebrush was full of millionaires who a year or so later were wondering about their next meal ticket or a free ride out of town" (Weight, 1972:32). Service to Rhyolite by the Las Vegas and Tonopah Railroad was discontinued in 1914, and in 1916 the Nevada Power Company cut off electricity.

Most businesses had shut down or moved by 1911, and the 1920 census found only 14 residents. A 1922 motor tour of Rhyolite by the *Los Angeles Times* found Rhyolite's only resident to be a 92-year-old man, who by 1924 had died.

As the town's few remaining buildings decayed and ghosts of faded dreams took up residence among the ruins, Hollywood used the picturesque site as a film location. For a 1925 movie, Paramount Pictures restored the famous Bottle House, built of an estimated 50,000 bottles during the town's peak. Orion Pictures used Rhyolite's ruins as the setting for its 1987 science-fiction movie "Cherry 2000," which depicted American society in collapse.

Production figures for the great Tonopah, Goldfield, and Rhyolite-Bullfrog booms between the time of their discovery and 1920 are revealing (Elliott, 1966:311). Tonopah is credited with production of more than $109 million; Goldfield, $80 million; and Rhyolite-Bullfrog lags far behind with only about $1.8 million. Clearly, Rhyolite was based more on a dream of economic wealth than on reality—that harsh arbitrator of the fate of boomtowns.

Rhyolite, the City of Golden Dreams, January 1908. Note the three-story John S. Cook Bank building in the center, the John T. Overbury building about a block to the left, and the concrete structure in the lower right-hand corner. Central Nevada Historical Society—Minnie Perchetti Collection

Bottle House, Rhyolite, undated (perhaps about 1910). The many saloons in desert mining towns produced large numbers of whiskey, beer, and wine bottles. These empties became a useful building material in an area where lumber was scarce and expensive. University of Nevada, Las Vegas—Dickinson Library Special Collections

Rhyolite, now the Ghost City of Golden Dreams, circa 1940. This photo is taken from approximately the same perspective as the photo on the opposite page. The ruins of the Cook and Overbury buildings are clearly visible as are the remains of the concrete structure in the lower right. That which is not carried off by others is inexorably reclaimed by the desert.

Looking up Golden Street toward the Las Vegas and Tonopah Railroad depot, Rhyolite, circa 1930. Note the John S. Cook and Overbury buildings on the left.

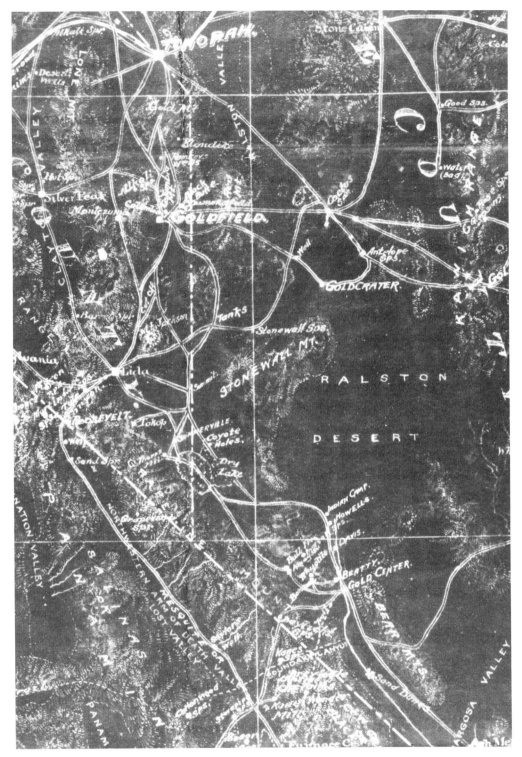

Portion of prospector's map made by Booker, Phellrick, and Fenner (1905) of Tonopah, Goldfield, Bullfrog, and principal mining districts. Note towns, roads, trails, and watering places in southern Nevada and the Death Valley region. University of Nevada, Las Vegas—Dickinson Library

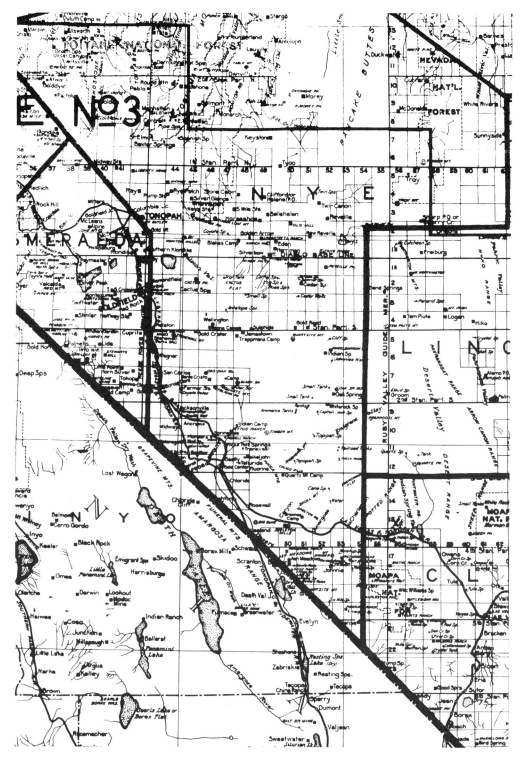

A portion of Clason's Guide Map of Nevada published by the Clason Map Co., Denver (1911). The map was produced for the Broadway Department Store, Los Angeles; the line across northern Nye and Lincoln counties reflects parcel post zone boundaries of the time. Most of southern Nevada was within zone 3, 150 to 300 miles from Los Angeles. Postage for a package was 7 cents per pound from zone 3. University of Nevada, Las Vegas—Dickinson Library Special Collections

Bob Montgomery kept his promise to build an elegant hotel in Beatty, the town he founded. The hotel's grand opening took place October 25, 1905; this photo was taken the next morning. At that time the Montgomery Hotel was one of the finest such establishments in the state of Nevada. The three cars in the front of the hotel had been driven from Goldfield for the opening.

CHAPTER FOUR

Beatty Beginnings

O f all the communities established in the Bullfrog area, Beatty had the best location. The site was relatively flat, and water could be obtained from wells drilled in the center of town at depths of less than 30 feet. But the promotion, in spring 1905, of the new nearby townsite of Rhyolite, just west of the Montgomery Shoshone Mine, drew settlers from adjoining communities.

Bob Montgomery Founds Beatty

If Bob Montgomery had not bought into the Beatty Township, it, too, might have become depopulated by the early exodus to Rhyolite. Montgomery's vow to build a grand hotel and make the town a milling center persuaded many Beatty residents not to join in the rush to Rhyolite. The town of Beatty was probably laid out in 1904 or early 1905. Montgomery filed the first plat map of the community, which contains the names of Beatty's first streets. The post office was established January 19, 1905.

Montgomery kept his promise to build a hotel in Beatty, and its construction probably played no small part in the consolidation of Beatty as a community. At a cost of $25,000, the hotel was the largest in the district at that time—indeed, one of the finest hotels in Nevada south of Reno. The grand opening of the Montgomery Hotel took place on October 25, 1905, with guests from as far away as Tonopah. A grand march was held, led by Mrs. Montgomery (who had come from San Francisco for the event) and Malcolm MacDonald, a Tonopah mining engineer and partner of Montgomery. (In 1909 the Montgomery Hotel was dismantled, moved to Pioneer, and renamed the Holland House; it later burned to the ground.)

In February 1906 (less than two years after he filed Beatty's plat map),

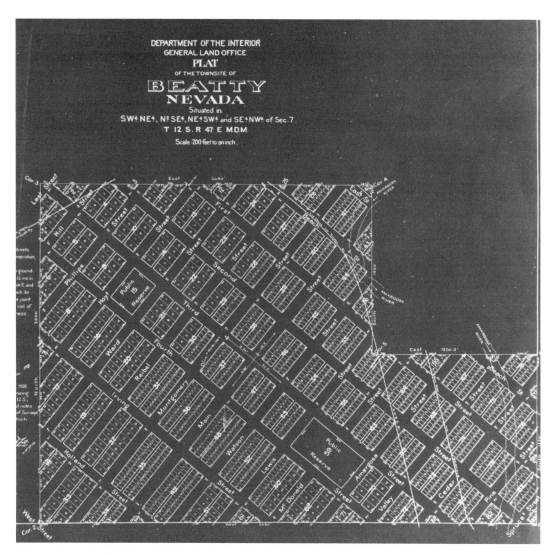

The original plat map of Beatty, accepted by the U.S. Department of Interior, General Land Office, Washington, D.C., June 26, 1908. Many of the present street names in Beatty were assigned in this survey. Montgomery Street is named after the town's founder, prospector, and mine operator, Ernest Alexander "Bob" Montgomery. Nevada Historical Society

Montgomery sold part of his Beatty properties, including the Montgomery Hotel, to Charles Schwab. But Schwab had no real interest in the Beatty holdings he had purchased from Montgomery, and shortly after the arrival of the Las Vegas and Tonopah Railroad, he sold them to Dr. William S. Phillips for a reported $100,000. Phillips, a con man known as the "little millionaire hustler from Chicago," proudly announced his plan to make Beatty the "Chicago of Nevada" (Lingenfelter, 1986:229). When Beatty's second railroad, the Bullfrog Goldfield, arrived in 1907, Phillips flamboyantly revealed his design to build a $100,000 hotel, a hospital, a city hall, a church, and so forth. He placed signs on vacant lots around the town where he planned to construct these buildings. He sold as many lots as he could,

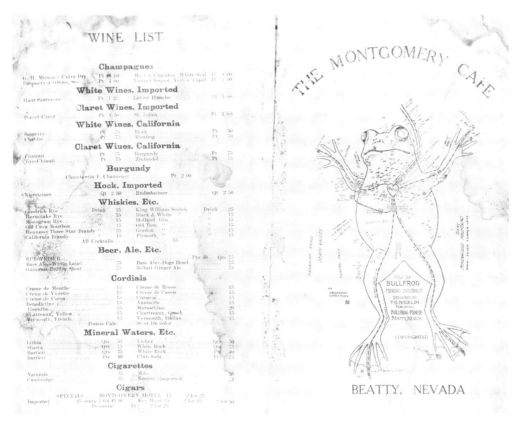

Front and back of the menu from the Montgomery Cafe, which was probably located in the Montgomery Hotel, Beatty, perhaps around 1907. The map, featuring a Bullfrog with Beatty as its heart, was designed by T. G. Nicklon, editor of the Bullfrog Miner *(later renamed the* Beatty Bullfrog Miner). *A good whiskey sold for 15 cents a drink, Budweiser Beer 40 cents a pint, and imported cigars 25 cents each or 3 for $1.00 [sic].* <small>Nye County History Project—Reidhead Collection</small>

then skipped town. Despite Schwab's lack of support for the town and Phillips' exploitative activities, the town survived its first years and was on its way to permanence on the Nevada map.

Hauling Freight by Horse and Railroad

The Bullfrog mining district was located in the middle of a vast little-explored wilderness, one of the most remote and inaccessible areas in the American West. Goldfield, the closest community of any consequence, was 65 miles to the north; Tonopah was about 90 miles away. Barren desert valleys separated by rugged mountain ranges lay to the east and west. Until the railroads arrived in the Bullfrog district in late 1906, the only way to get in or out of the area was by horsepower or on foot. By early June 1905, nearly 1500 horses were engaged in hauling freight from Las Vegas to Bullfrog, and 50 freighters would daily pass each other on the road. Teams of 6, 12, 16, and 20 horses or mules were used. Roads were little more than a deep wagon track filled with a fine dust. A speedy rate of travel was 2 miles per hour. The trip to Bullfrog from Las Vegas took a

"The First Snow"
Beatty, Bullfrog District, Nevada, Nov. 20, 1905.

Beatty, looking west toward Rhyolite, November 20, 1905. Note the Montgomery Hotel.
Central Nevada Historical Society—Nevada Historical Society

Beatty, looking northeast, 1906.
University of Nevada, Las Vegas—Dickinson Library Special Collections

The first Decoration Day, Beatty, 1906; looking east. All persons unidentified. National Park Service—Death Valley National Monument

The first ice plant in Beatty, probably 1905. Ice was a valuable commodity for pioneers on the Beatty frontier. Ice made cold drinks possible and could keep food from spoiling. National Park Service—Death Valley National Monument

Northern Saloon, Beatty, Nevada, 1906. Burros were clearly loved and appreciated by the residents of this frontier oasis. National Park Service—Death Valley National Monument

Hauling freight near Beatty. University of Nevada, Las Vegas—Dickinson Library Special Collections

Las Vegas and Tonopah Railroad depot, Beatty, undated. Nye County Town History Project—Lemmon Collection

week. After leaving Las Vegas, freighters camped the first night at Tule Springs at the north end of the Las Vegas Valley; the second night was spent at Indian Springs. Water was available at both camps. The third night was spent at a dry camp between Indian Springs and Ash Meadows. The fourth night was at a wet camp at Ash Meadows. The trip into Beatty took another two or three days; all those nights were spent at dry camps.

Of the three railroads that eventually connected in Beatty, the first to arrive was Senator William A. Clark's Las Vegas and Tonopah Railroad (LV&T). Fully scheduled service from Las Vegas to Beatty began on October 22, 1906, and Beatty celebrated by officially designating October 22 and 23 as Railroad Days. The Beatty depot of the LV&T was located at the southeastern edge of town between Second Street and Third Street. The line's boardinghouse was constructed along the tracks to the north near the end of Second Street. The LV&T passed through

Beatty to the north, circling first to Rhyolite, then on to Goldfield. It ceased operations after twelve years, in October 1918.

The second railroad to reach Beatty was the Bullfrog Goldfield Railroad (BG), which arrived April 25, 1907. It was financed by a syndicate that involved many prominent Philadelphians, including John Brock, who had major mining holdings in Tonopah and had been behind construction of the Tonopah and Goldfield

Tonopah and Tidewater Railroad car. Beatty, late 1930s. Nye County Town History Project—Reidhead Collection

Tonopah and Tidewater Railroad Engine No. 8, Beatty, probably late 1930s. Nye County History Project—Reidhead Collection

Tonopah and Tidewater Railroad as it crossed the Amargosa River about 8 or 10 miles from Tecopa, California, circa 1915. Trestles like the one on the right were very expensive to build.
Nye County Town History Project—Crowell Collection

Railroad. At Goldfield it connected with the Tonopah and Goldfield Railroad, which ran on to Tonopah. South of Goldfield, stations included Keith, Stella, Cuprite, Wagner, San Carlos, Bonnie Claire, Jacksonville, Ancram, Springdale, Hot Springs, and Beatty. The BG traveled south through Beatty, passed through the Beatty Narrows, and circled round the south end of the Bullfrog Hills to Rhyolite. After 1914, the Bullfrog Goldfield Railroad used the Las Vegas and Tonopah tracks from a point just south of Bonnie Claire to Goldfield, with the other tracks between Rhyolite and Goldfield being abandoned. The BG lasted until January 1928, when its last train departed from Beatty. Because it duplicated service provided by the LV&T, Myrick (1963:505) called it, "Without a doubt, . . . Nevada's most unwanted railroad."

Borax Smith's Tonopah and Tidewater Railroad (T&T) reached Beatty on October 27, 1907. Technically the T&T Railroad did not go into Beatty but went only as far as Gold Center; it then used the Bullfrog Goldfield's railroad tracks to travel on through the Beatty Narrows and into Beatty. All operations on the T&T ceased on June 14, 1940. On the fate of the T&T's materials, Myrick wrote:

On July 18, 1942, contractors Sharp and Fellows began tearing up the rails at Beatty and, working southward, the job was completed all the way to Ludlow by July 25, 1943. Of the residue, a quantity of bridge timbers ended up as part of the Apple Valley Inn at Apple Valley, while the ties became scattered all over, a large number being used in the building of the El Rancho Motel in Barstow. Two of the locomotives went to the Kaiser Steel Plant at Fontana, California, while a third went to the San Bernardino Air Base (Myrick, 1963:593).

J. Irving Crowell and the Chloride Cliff Mine

J. Irving Crowell arrived in Beatty in 1905 after a three-day trip by horse and buggy from Las Vegas. He was originally from New England and had been raised on Cape Cod. His wife, Annie, a Canadian, remained in the couple's home in Los Angeles while Crowell was on the desert seeking his fortune as a mining promoter.

The Chloride Cliff Mine, located near the crest of the Funeral Mountains almost due west of Beatty and south of Daylight Pass, had originally been discovered by August J. Franklin, a man named Hanson, and Beatty pioneer Eugene Lander in August 1871. The company Franklin and his partners formed was disbanded, but Franklin continued to hold the property until his death in 1904, when his son George took it over. Activity at the nearby Keane Wonder Mine led to revived interest in the immediate area, and prior to the Panic of 1907, J. Irving Crowell purchased an interest in the Chloride Cliff Mine from George Franklin for an estimated $110,000.

After his initial purchase, Crowell obtained backing from investors in Pennsylvania and reopened the mine under the banner of the Penn Mining and Leasing Company in the fall of 1909. Crowell found gold-bearing rock assaying at better than $35 a ton and constructed a 1-stamp mill at the foot of the mine dump. Some ore was shipped, and at one point Crowell attempted unsuccessfully to sell his holdings to investors in England. Crowell maintained a residence on the property until 1917. Crowell's son, J. Irving Crowell, Jr., said that his father never made a lot of money on the Chloride Cliff Mine but that some leasers did fairly well (J. and M-K. Crowell, 1987).

The Crowells' Fluorspar Mine

In 1917 a man named Bill Kennedy was prospecting on Bare Mountain. He threw down his pick and broke loose a piece of soft, purple rock. The next day he happened to meet J. I. Crowell and showed him a specimen. Crowell recognized the sample as fluorspar (calcium fluoride), and he purchased the information on the formation's location for $500 cash. Following Kennedy's directions, Crowell went to the site, staked out a claim, and filed a location notice. He named his new claim the Daisy. Over the years several other claims were added to what is now sometimes referred to as the Daisy Group (J. I. and D. Crowell, 1987).

Originally Crowell's interest in the Daisy focused on gold prospects rather than fluorspar, the presence of which was believed to be a favorable indication that gold-bearing ore existed at lower levels. Fluorspar was much less glamorous than gold and was used primarily as a catalyst in the production of steel; it has the effect of making molten slag thinner and more fluid. Although Crowell did not find gold at his Daisy mine, the property has proven to be a solid producer of fluorspar; it was the longest continuously operated mine in the Beatty–Death Valley area.

In 1923, personal misfortune struck Crowell on the T&T. Because of a railroad engineer's misjudgment, Crowell was thrown head-first through a partition and

J. Irving Crowell at his desk in the dugout dwelling he called home at his mine at Chloride Cliff. Crowell possessed a camera with a high-quality lens, accounting for the detail. Judging from the days marked off the calendar behind him, this photo was taken October 12, 1915. A clock on the wall in a portion of the photo cropped away indicates the time was 9:27 (presumably A.M. because the camera did not have a flash attachment). The ruins of Crowell's dugout home are still visible at Chloride Cliff.

Crowells' mill located at Chloride Cliff in the Funeral Mountains, circa 1915. The mill, under construction, is seen completed in the next photo. It was designed to process ore by the cyanide and amalgamation methods, but only small amounts of ore were ever run through it.

J. Irving Crowell's mine at Chloride Cliff, circa 1915. Crowell and his associates constructed the buildings in the foreground, known to them and the workers as "New Camp." Nye County History Project—Crowell Collection

Surface structures and trucks at Crowells' fluorspar mine located on Bare Mountain east of Beatty, circa 1928. The surface structures belie the mine's extensive underground workings and its long record of production and of providing employment to Beatty area miners. The truck on the left is a Model-T; the other is a Model-A. Nye County Town History Project—Crowell Collection

Panoramic view of Beatty, circa 1915. The view is of the Bullfrog Hills to the west and the Funeral Mountains in the distance. Note the location of Chloride Cliff. The road exiting town to the west in the middle of the photo leads to Rhyolite and on to Daylight Pass in the Funeral Mountains. Nye County Town History Project—Crowell Collection

Panoramic view of Beatty, looking east, circa 1915. Note the Exchange Club (the white building on the left) behind the water tower. Beatty Mountain is in the center; Bare Mountain is on the far right. Nye County Town History Project—Crowell Collection

J. Irving Crowell, Jr., as a child, at Candelaria, Nevada, 1903. His mother, Annie L. Crowell, is standing on the right; others unidentified. Nye County Town History Project—Crowell Collection

was severely injured. He was an invalid for months. He partially recovered, but never was able to do physical labor again. Because of his injuries, Crowell was forced to close the fluorspar mine temporarily, and the fate of his son, J. Irving Crowell, Jr., who was only a year away from graduation from Stanford University, was forever changed. The younger Crowell was forced to withdraw from Stanford because of deteriorating family finances. After a short stint at the less expensive University of California at Los Angeles, he got a job in the booming southern California steel industry at U.S. Steel's plant in Torrance. Several years later, a comment by a fellow worker whom he respected caused him to alter the course of his life. The fellow worker told him he was "a plain damn fool" for working for others if he had a fluorspar mine. Crowell did some checking into the market for fluorspar in southern California, and after receiving assurances that U.S. Steel, and later Bethlehem Steel, would purchase his fluorspar, he returned to Beatty in 1927 to work the mine.

Upon his return to Beatty in 1927, Crowell, Jr., and Louis Vidano, a former employee at the Chloride Cliff Mine who had faithfully remained in touch with the family, worked the fluorspar mine. The two men drilled and blasted by day and hoisted a few buckets of ore to the surface before going home at day's end. Crowell would return to town, eat, and then go back to the mine and work a second shift, climbing down the 134-foot shaft, filling a bucket with the purple ore, then climbing to the surface to hoist the ore and dump it. Then he would repeat the tedious, slow process. This he did until about 10 o'clock every night, seven days a week.

Except for sporadic shutdowns during some of the worst years of the Depression in the 1930s, the Crowell fluorspar mine operated almost continuously between 1927 and 1989, producing in excess of 200,000 tons. It was a steady source of employment for a handful of miners, and at times employment peaked at 15 to 20 men. The ore pinches in and out, and the workings have varied over the years from only 6 inches to 70 or 80 feet in width. The small dump (where waste rock is disposed of) belies the mine's longevity because the Crowells have almost always dug on shipping-grade rock.

In 1928, Crowell married his Los Angeles sweetheart, Dorothy. The couple raised a family in Beatty, where they were residents until Dorothy's death in 1990. J. Irving, Jr., passed away in 1991.

Conclusion

The town of Beatty was created by the excitement of the Bullfrog-Rhyolite boom, which was based on the hope that the gold deposits in the Bullfrog Hills were both rich and deep. They were neither. Rhyolite and all the other small communities it spawned faded almost as quickly as they began. Beatty, however, had something going for it—location. In their history of Rhyolite, Harold and Lucile Weight wrote, "Beatty . . . was on the natural, shortest, best-watered route between Goldfield and Las Vegas. Any main road, any railroad, was certain to go that way—as the highway goes today" (Weight, 1972:14). Beatty's accessibility and water supply made it possible for the small community to get through the first few years that are so critical in determining whether a Western boomtown will survive. Once a nucleus at Beatty had proven that it could survive after 1910, the town became the economic and social center for a very large geographical area.

Looking northeast up Main Street, Beatty, circa 1922. The Exchange Club is visible on the right of the photo. The growth of the evergreen tree just to the left of the light pole can be monitored in pictures of Beatty through the years. Nye County Town History Project—Palsgrove Collection

CHAPTER FIVE

The Late 1920s to World War II

Like the desert flowers in the spring, the two-score or more of towns that formed in the wake of the heat and excitement of the Bullfrog boom seemed to appear almost overnight out of the rocky soil—only to disappear nearly as quickly. Each town's emergence was heralded as the beginning of something important, and at the time, it seemed as though all would last forever. It was not to be. The veins of precious metal in the barren mountains that fed each town were as thin and unpredictable as the desert rains that watered the blossoms of spring. Like the flowers, the towns would not endure long. They would have their colorful moments in the sun, and then they would disappear into the rocky desert soil from which they sprang.

There was one exception: Beatty. As the other towns faded, it hung on. Situated about half-way between Las Vegas and Tonopah on the main north-south roadway in Nevada, and with plenty of readily accessible water, Beatty, though it remained small, became the economic nucleus for a vast area that encompassed more than 50 miles in any direction in southern Nevada and the eastern California desert region.

Economic activity in Beatty in the late 1920s and early 1930s included some mining, an assortment of local merchants, the distribution of oil and gas, the construction of Death Valley Scotty's Castle during the late 1920s, and the production and sale of illegal alcohol during Prohibition.

By the late 1930s, mining activity in Beatty had increased somewhat in comparison to the level of a few years earlier. The Roosevelt administration had raised the price of gold, which stimulated a number of small operations in central

Workers unloading a ball mill for use at the Gold Ace Mine, located south of Beatty, probably early 1930s. Nye County Town History Project—Palsgrove Collection

Nevada. As the only community of consequence in a vast area, Beatty was a natural trade center for the miners. Ralph Lisle remembered the mining activity at Skidoo and Pioneer, with 20 or 30 men working at Bullfrog and a few less at Rhyolite. There was also activity at other area mines—the Keane Wonder, the Chloride Cliff, the Ubehebe, the Gold Ace, the Panama on Bare Mountain, and the Diamond Queen; in 1940 the payroll at Carrara frequently reached 200 (R. and C. Lisle, 1987).

The Reverts Boost the Beatty Economy

The Revert family was typical of many that came to Nevada and made contributions to the economy. Albert Revert, patriarch of the Revert family of Beatty, was born in Le Havre, France, September 20, 1869; when he was a young child, he immigrated to the United States with his family. The Reverts first lived in New York City, but when Albert's mother died, he and his father made their way to San Francisco and later to Virginia City, where young Albert attended the Fourth Ward School. At age eleven he found a job working in a box factory in nearby Verdi, and he lived with a French family there (A. Revert, 1987).

Albert moved to Tonopah shortly after the great silver boom began in 1900. By this time, Revert had mastered every aspect of the lumber business, and he established a lumber yard on the north side of town at the site of the old Conley Yard. His Tonopah Lumber Company (which owned a large number of horses, mules, and wagons) hauled lumber from Mina to Tonopah prior to construction of the railroad. It was one of several firms that transported supplies. In all, 400 horses in teams of 12 to 20 were involved.

Albert Revert, patriarch of the Revert family, circa 1935. Revert was in his late 50s or early 60s when this photo was taken. Nye County Town History Project—Revert Collection

Formerly known as the Palmer Store, the Amargosa Cattle Company Store was renamed by the Reverts when Albert Revert purchased it as part of the Shirk Estate shortly after he and his family moved to Beatty in 1929. University of Nevada, Las Vegas—Dickinson Library Special Collections

Revert married Henrietta Bucking, a San Francisco woman whose parents had come from Germany. Their first child, Art, was born in San Francisco in late 1905 and shortly thereafter—not long after the great San Francisco earthquake—mother and baby joined Albert in Tonopah: The family resided in Tonopah for several years.

Albert eventually became the owner of a large sawmill in Verdi and a string of lumber yards in virtually every community of consequence in Nevada, including Fallon, Sparks, Elko, and Reno. With profits from his Tonopah Lumber Company, Revert purchased the Verdi Lumber Company in 1908 from Oliver Lonkey. After completing high school, Art joined his father in the lumber business in Verdi, working at general duties, including grading lumber. Times were good for the company, but a number of serious fires proved to be the company's undoing. There was one during World War I, which was believed to have been set by a German agent. Another fire in the 1920s was caused by a whirlwind that scattered hot coals over the mill area.

After the Reverts' lumber business was wiped out, the family looked around the state for, as Art said, "a place to land" (A. Revert, 1987). Albert and son Art arrived in Beatty on New Year's Eve, 1929. They chose Beatty because a mine at Chloride Cliff looked promising. The unexpected deaths of two of the three investors led to the failure of the enterprise. Revert then decided to purchase the Shirk estate from Shirk's daughter, for approximately $10,000. The estate included the old Beatty Ranch, consisting of 300 acres, the stone cabin once occupied by Old Man Beatty, and considerable water rights; a primitive community water system that obtained water from the Beatty Ranch and supplied it to a small number of town residents; a number of pieces of property in town; and a store, known as the

Looking west down Main Street, Beatty, probably late 1930s. The California Hotel is on the left side of the street. University of Nevada, Las Vegas—Dickinson Library Special Collections

Amargosa Land and Cattle Company (sometimes called Palmer's Store, after a former owner), housed in a large, iron-clad building at the north end of town.

The store, renamed the Revert Mercantile, was the largest in town. It carried anything a person in an isolated desert community could possibly need: a variety of canned goods; fresh meat that was shipped in by rail from Ottumwa, Iowa; mining supplies, including picks, shovels, drilling steel, and dynamite and caps (stored in a powder house on the hill east of town). Revert did big business in the sale of coal, which was brought in on the railroad by the carload and sold by the sack.

Other Economic Activity

In addition to Revert Mercantile, there were two other stores in town: one owned by the Richings family (operated by "Mom" Richings) and the other by Cy Johnson. H. H. ("Pop") Richings operated the Standard Oil dealership. Beatty had its share of bars, including the Gold Ace, St. Peters' Bar (run by Glen St. Peters), and the Exchange Club (originally built and still being run at that time by George Greenwood). The Gold Ace burned down about 1940—many residents remembered the fire. Joe Andre's Silver Diner and a fountain in the Exchange Club were popular restaurants.

The T&T Railroad employed several townspeople in Beatty. Before the roads in and out of town were paved, nearly all goods came into town from the south on the railroad. Dave Aspen was then the railroad agent; he had originally worked in Tonopah for the railroad.

A highway sign being readied at the Beatty Auto Court in the early 1930s for eventual placement about 30 miles south on Highway 95 in the vicinity of Lathrop Wells (Amargosa Valley). This photo is particularly valuable because it provides a listing of many of the business establishments and services available in Beatty at that time. Nye County Town History Project—Lisle Collection

*Pop (left) and Mom (center) Richings and Death Valley Scotty (right) in front of the Richings'
Beatty Store, early 1930s.* Nye County Town History Project—Thompson Collection

*The interior of the Richings' Beatty Store, circa 1935. The lovely Indian baskets on display,
probably made by local Beatty Shoshone Indians, would be quite valuable today. Mineral
specimens and old "purple bottles" are visible on the shelves and in the display cases.* Nye County
Town History Project—Thompson Collection

Main Street, Beatty, looking northeast, probably 1920s. The Exchange Club is visible in the right foreground as is Richings' Store in the left foreground. Note the evergreen tree on the right side of the street. University of Nevada, Las Vegas—Dickinson Library Special Collections

Main Street, Beatty, looking northeast, probably late 1940s. The Exchange Club is visible in the foreground on the right. Richings' Store is gone. The evergreen just down the street from the Exchange Club has grown. University of Nevada, Las Vegas—Dickinson Library Special Collections

Lisle Contributes to Beatty's Transportation Economy

The widespread availability of the automobile added a new dimension to transportation and economic activity in southcentral Nevada. Though the automobile clearly had its advantages in the area, the conveniently scheduled railroad service at first provided stiff competition to the horseless carriage as the mode of travel between the region's widely separated towns. However, as railroad schedules were first reduced and then gradually eliminated entirely, the

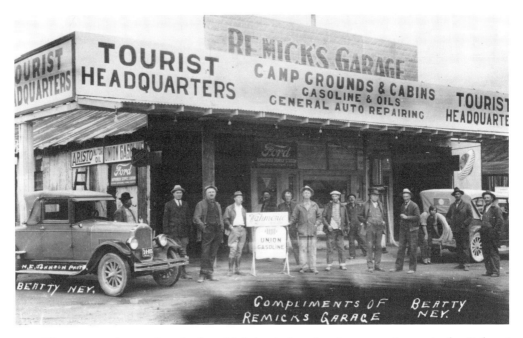

Providing automotive services, food, and lodging to travelers became an increasingly vital part of the Beatty economy during the 1930s. This garage was located at the corner of Second and Main, directly across the street from the Exchange Club. Nye County Town History Project—Palsgrove Collection

Regular bus service for the communities between Las Vegas and Reno was provided by the Las Vegas–Tonopah–Reno Stages (LTR). The company was founded by the Mikulich family; and for many years, especially after the closure of the Tonopah and Tidewater Railroad in 1940, the service was a vital transportation link. Pictured is an LTR bus from the 1930s.

Nevada Historical Society

Beatty resident Chloe Colvin (who later married Ralph Lisle) and Red Mills in front of the barbershop, Main Street, Beatty, about 1932. Chloe was taking hair-cutting lessons at the shop at the time; Red Mills, Homer and Vic Ritter, and Chloe's brother, Sam Colvin, served as practice subjects for Chloe.

automobile came into its own. It emerged as the transportation means of choice (the only alternatives were foot, horse or burro, and wagon).

The growing popularity of the automobile created new economic opportunities in Beatty as well as other communities. Service stations—as they were properly termed in those days—were opened to meet motorists' needs for gas, tires, repairs, directions, and a friendly word. Service stations gradually became an important factor in Beatty's economy and continue to contribute significantly.

Many, including Ralph Lisle, saw economic opportunity in the automobile's arrival. Ralph Lisle, the son of John Quincy and Celesta Fairbanks Lisle, was the grandson of Ralph J. "Dad" Fairbanks, a southern Nevada–Mojave Desert pioneer and town builder. Lisle was born in Fernley, Nevada, in 1914, but spent most of his life in the Beatty–Death Valley area (R. and C. Lisle, 1987).

After Ralph Lisle graduated from high school, he worked for two years for his grandfather, "Dad" Fairbanks in Baker, California, and for seven years for his uncle, Charlie Brown, in Shoshone, California. Working for Fairbanks and Brown amounted to a quality apprenticeship in the management and operation of gas stations and general stores in the Death Valley region. In 1938, Brown sent Lisle to Beatty to reactivate the Standard Oil distributorship, which had closed down early in the Depression, and the service station that they had recently purchased from H. H. Richings. (The other distributorship—Union Oil—was owned by the Reverts.)

Lisle and his wife, Chloe (whom he had married in 1939), operated the station until the outbreak of World War II, when both the distributorship and station were deemed a nonessential industry and were forced to close. Lisle switched to the mining of minerals that were considered essential for the war effort, which did not include gold. Later he entered military service. After the war, he returned home and found that the ownership of the Standard Oil distributorship had been transferred in his absence. Later, the Lisles opened a Union 76 station on Second Street across from the Exchange Club.

Scotty's Castle: "Neither of Us Pays Rent"

Construction of Scotty's Castle, which began in 1925, had a notable effect on Beatty, the closest town to the site. Walter Edward Scott, better known as Death Valley Scotty, was born in Cyanthiana, Kentucky, on September 20, 1872, and came to Nevada at the age of fourteen; he became skilled as a cowhand and at bronco busting. After a stint with Buffalo Bill Cody's Wild West Show, he ended up in the Death Valley area where he put his greatest talents to use—as a quintessential flimflam man. Richard Lingenfelter described Scotty as "a ham actor, a conscienceless con man, an almost pathological liar, and a charismatic bullslinger" (1986:242). Scotty would do almost anything for attention and publicity and could pry a dollar out of the most tight-fisted businessman. Scotty's Castle—probably his greatest con—involved Albert M. Johnson, a wealthy capitalist from Chicago. Johnson, the son of an Oberlin, Ohio, banker, had graduated from Cornell University in 1895. He began amassing his own wealth by speculating in the Missouri zinc mining boom with money borrowed from his father. He eventually acquired control of the National Life Insurance Company in 1902.

Walter Edward ("Death Valley Scotty") Scott pictured with two mules at "his" ranch in lower Grapevine Canyon, circa 1929. National Park Service—Death Valley National Monument

"SCOTTY" AND WIFE AS THEY APPEARED AT BEATTY, NEV.

Death Valley Scotty and his wife, Ella Josephine, in Beatty, 1906. There is little mention of her in accounts of his life. University of Nevada, Las Vegas—Dickinson Library Special Collections

Unloading the last car of materials for the construction of Death Valley Scotty's Castle from the railroad at Bonnie Claire, Nevada, January 7, 1928. National Park Service—Death Valley National Monument

Construction of the main building of Scotty's Castle, April 24, 1927. National Park Service—Death Valley National Monument

Undated postcard photo showing Death Valley Scotty's Castle and guest house. Nevada Historical Society

An old postcard photo showing Albert and Bessie Johnson with Death Valley Scotty at Scotty's Castle, circa 1935. Nevada Historical Society

Undated postcard photo showing the music room at Death Valley Scotty's Castle.
Nevada Historical Society

An article in the *Beatty Bulletin* gave Scotty's version of how he persuaded Johnson to underwrite the construction of a great mansion at the mouth of Grapevine Canyon at the north end of Death Valley.

I always wanted a castle in Death Valley, so one time, several years ago, when I was in Chicago I thought I'd see about getting it. I noticed a huge skyscraper and asked a policeman who owned it.

"That belongs to a big insurance company," he said. I asked him who the head man was, and he replied, "The president, of course, A. M. Johnson."

So I got in the elevator and rode to the top floor where I asked for Mr. Johnson. He was very cordial, and inquired, "What can I do for you, young man?"

"I live in the desert and want to build a Castle," I told him. "I figure it should cost about a million and a half dollars. I thought maybe you'd give it to me."

"Why, of course," Johnson said, going to his safe. Then he stopped and remarked, "I'm not sure a million and a half is enough. Better take two million."

"So I took the two million and came out here and built the Castle," Scotty concluded straight-faced ("District Loses True Friend in Death of A. M. Johnson," 1948).

The castle, called "one of the wonders of the world," was featured in the *Saturday Evening Post*, and for eighteen days stories about it appeared on the front page of the *Los Angeles Record*. The castle became so famous that it even upstaged Scotty, who refused to sleep in his $40,000 bedroom in the castle, preferring a small bungalow several miles down the canyon, or if the Johnsons were not there, sleeping on a cot amid dirty dishes and pans in the kitchen (Lingenfelter, 1986:461–463). The mansion, located in the middle of nowhere, had its own water supply, sewer system, hydroelectric generator, cold storage, ice plant, air conditioning, and solar heating. Interior work was accomplished by European artisans and craftsmen. Johnson furnished the building with custom and antique items obtained from extended buying trips. When it was completed, the castle boosted Beatty's economy by becoming a major tourist attraction.

As Lingenfelter (1986:461) has pointed out, Death Valley Scotty was the personification of Death Valley for many years, a major attraction in himself, as fascinating as the mountains and the valley whose name he bore as a nickname. Scotty had always had a flair for cultivating publicity. Though Johnson put up the estimated $2.5 million for the castle, Johnson was more than content to let Scotty give the world the impression that it was Scotty's, constructed with Scotty's millions.

In much the same vein, the story is told of the persistent tourist who wanted to know definitely who owned the Castle, Johnson or Scotty. Ever a master of evasion, Mr. Johnson replied:

"Well, my friend, it's like this. Scotty lives here and I live here, and neither of us pays rent" ("District Loses True Friend in Death of A. M. Johnson," 1948).

Death Valley Scotty died in January 1954, six years after his benefactor. In the obituary in the *Beatty Bulletin*, Scotty was described as one of the last remaining links with the early West: "Death overtook him on Nevada soil, where in his younger days he wrote so many colorful chapters in the state's history." He is buried on a hill near the castle that bears his name ("Scotty Buried on Hill Near Famed Castle," 1954).

GOLDFIELD NEWS
AND
The BEATTY BULLETIN

Vol. 44. No. 16   GOLDFIELD NEVADA FRIDAY, JANUARY 16, 1948   PRICE: TEN CENTS

Everyone Invited To Goldfield on Independence Day

ELKS LODGE PLANS BIG CELEBRATION TO MARK JULY 4

John Brawley, exalted ruler of the Goldfield Elks, this week issued an invitation to all residents of Beatty and surrounding area to spend July 4 in Goldfield, where a big Independence Day celebration, outstripping that of last year, will be held.

"We're planning an entire day of entertainment, including a free barbecue late in the afternoon, and we hope that all of our good friends in Beatty will respond as they did last year by coming up to Goldfield and sharing in the fun," the Exalted Ruler said.

Beatty residents who accepted a similar invitation from the Goldfield Elks last year (and virtually everyone living here did) will not hesitate long in saying "We'll be there for sure!" Chief among their activities, of course, will be some loud rooting for the Beatty softball team, which will be out to avenge last year's one-run setback at the hands of Goldfield.

This year's celebration will be bigger and better than ever, with several events added to the day's program. In addition to races for young and old, there will be a spirited tug-of-war between the best "muscle men" of Beatty and Goldfield.

Beatty mining men will also be eligible to enter the drilling and mucking contests which it is hoped can be staged in Goldfield this year. Plans are being made to haul a huge rock to the corner of Ramsey and Columbia

SEVEN GRADUATES RECEIVE DIPLOMAS WEDNESDAY NIGHT

Graduation exercises for both the high school and grammar school were held Wednesday night in Town hall. Those graduating from the elementary school were Carol Weeks, Loretta Gordon, Donald Crowell, Carl Looney and Florence Pulliam. Nadine Russell and Dolores Strozzi were the high school graduates.

The stage was decorated in the school colors of green and white and a huge 1948 was strung across the front of the stage, making a lovely background for the graduates and guest speakers, including District Attorney William Crowell from Tonopah, Neal Cook and Barton Riggs of the school board, and Fred Dees, the principal.

The program was as follows: Florence Pulliam, Class History; Loretta Gordon, Piano Solo—Starlight Walz; Carl Looney, Class Prophecy; Carol Weeks, Piano Solo—Fairies Harp; Nadine Crowell, Class Will; Nadine Russell, Speech on Americanism.

Mr. Crowell delivered the main address to the graduates and praised Miss Russell very highly on the splendid manner in which her talk was given and the unusual theories contained in her address.

Mr. Dees invited the public to the annual school picnic that was held Thursday at the Gibson ranch.

Mr. Riggs gave a vote of thanks to the teachers for their work this year and for the years of faithful service that Mr. Dees and Mr. Davis have given. Both teachers are resigning this year.

THREE-PIECE LAS VEGAS

Cast Ready for May 29 Minstrel

Finishing touches are being put on the rollicking minstrel show which local talent will present at the Town hall in Beatty next Saturday night May 29, beginning at 8 p. m. The large cast has been rehearsing diligently for several weeks, and pronounces itself ready to take the stage.

One of the highlights of the revue will be a novel Hawaiian dance routine headed by Renee Gibson with a cast of nine. Included will be an authentic chant of the islands, based on an ancient fishing ritual built around the story of Kaelanna on the Isle of Kalia. This story tells of a boy and a girl who embarked on calm waters in their canoe, only to be caught up by a sudden storm.

The music stems from the watchers on the beach, and later the feasting and rejoicing when the young couple are saved. There are two other sequences, all in the Hawaiian mood, and a hula dance that accompanies the opening chant.

Many other features and specialties will be included in the show as well as the traditional repartee between the interlocutor and end men.

CIGARS ARE ON NORM; WIFE HAS BABY BOY

Mr. and Mrs. Norman Revert are the proud parents of a son born Saturday evening around 8 p. m. at the hospital in Henderson. The baby boy is the second child of the Reverts. They have a daughter, Virginia, who will be 10 years old in

BROWNIE INCREASES STAFF BUT RETAINS SAME COLOR SCHEME

There was more reason than ever this week to call it Brownie's store, as the popular proprietor of Beatty's famed "one-stop shopping center" added a new Brown to the store's personnel—Arthur K. Brown, formerly of Boulder City.

The newcomer does not go by the nickname of Brownie, but is called Art, so no confusion is anticipated from this source.

Art brings with him a well-rounded knowledge of the grocery and meat business, acquired through seven years association with the Market Spot Wholesale & Retail store in Las Vegas. He previously worked for Albert Steinfield in Tacoma, Ariz.

Art is a former serviceman, having been a member of the U. S. Engineers for some time. He and Mrs. Brown have their home in Boulder City, but will make their residence in Beatty as soon as Mrs. Brown returns from Tacoma, Wash., where she is visiting her son.

OPERATION FOLLOWS SEIZURE BY BILLY PRUITT WHILE RIDING

Billy Emelin Pruitt was taken seriously ill late last week while branding cattle for the Fitzgeralds. Billy is the youngest son of Mr. and Mrs. Jack Pruitt, and really has the stamina and a lot of "what it takes" for all of his 17 years.

While riding out by the Ma 3 windmill about 23 miles from Beatty, Billy was seized with severe abdominal pains but had presence of mind enough to leave the branding irons in Ross Long's truck so that the work

SECRET GOLD HOARD HIDDEN AT CASTLE?

No Trace Found of Rich Cache Owned by Johnson

WHAT HAPPENED TO 7500 OZ. GOLD DUST TREASURE TROVE AFTER JOHNSON DIED?

A secret cache of over 7500 oz. of gold dust valued at about a quarter of a million dollars, remains unaccounted for in the will and behests of A. M. Johnson, wealthy Los Angeles philanthropist and religious zealot, who died last January, the News-Bulletin learned this week. The possible existence of the modern "pot of gold" was disclosed by Walter Scott (Death Valley Scotty) and confirmed by executive personnel of Scotty's

Castle, 60 miles from Beatty and Goldfield, who said that they knew of the treasure trove before Johnson's death but had no inkling as to its present whereabouts.

Scotty averred that two years ago Johnson made a trip to his ranch, located a short distance from the Castle, and produced several bags of almost pure gold dust which he had accumulated through the years. Where it came from Scotty could not say, and Johnson was reluctant about telling him.

The two men secretly weighed the precious material, finding that it totaled slightly over 7512 oz., according to Scotty. Later, Johnson mentioned the matter to Mr. and Mrs. Henry Rings, who manage the Castle and indicated that he was puzzled as to how he would ultimately dispose of the gold.

Johnson, a meticulous man, had carefully provided for the disposition of virtually every article of his worldly goods before his death, but nowhere was there any mention made of the quarter of a million dollars' worth of gold dust. Scotty said

Since Johnson had endeavored to take him into his confidence on matters of importance, Scotty is puzzled to know what became of the treasure, and indicates that he has encouraged a private search...

FRIENDS SURPRISE RENEE GIBSON WITH BIRTHDAY SUPPER

Mrs. Bob Gibson was feted by a group of friends that journeyed to the Gibson ranch Sunday afternoon. It was Mrs. Gibson's birthday and she was honored at a surprise picnic supper.

After the beautiful presents were opened and supper was served the guests were conducted on a tour of the grounds.

In 10 years, the couple has built one of the most attractive places in the desert. There are now 19 buildings on the ranch, including chicken houses, feed houses, wash house, dressing rooms for the swimming pool, and the new housing units built recently for tourist accommodations.

The ranch consists of 140 acres, 20 acres on each side of

Growth and Improvements

According to the U.S. Census for 1940, Beatty was still quite small. The population of the township, which included those who lived in the area from Springdale, located at the head of Oasis Valley, to Lathrop Wells, now known as Amargosa Valley, was 450; most lived in Beatty. Ralph Lisle remembered there was no housing—not even a trail—west of Montgomery Street, "just sagebrush and rocks." Quite a number of houses had been moved in from Rhyolite and Pioneer. Big cottonwood trees lined the wooden sidewalks of Main Street, and the fronts of many buildings had canopies. The trees, the canopies, and the wooden sidewalks were removed during the 1950s when the State Highway Department paved the road through Beatty and widened it in the process.

Until about 1940, Beatty had no electricity. The first supplier, Jim Mardis, obtained a franchise and provided a few families with electricity. This system frequently broke down, never ran on a regular schedule, and could not be depended upon for refrigeration. About 1940, the Reverts obtained a government loan, bought out Mardis, and expanded the system. The new supplier, known as the Amargosa Power Company, bought four big International diesel engines equipped with 50-kilowatt generators, scrounged the desert for poles, and wired the town. Anybody who wanted electricity could sign up. The availability of electricity in Beatty allowed many people to purchase refrigerators. In 1950, street lights were installed in Beatty, first on Main Street and then on some of the side streets. Prior to that the only light after dark was from shops and stores open after sundown.

The Amargosa Power Company operated until April 1963, when the Nevada Public Service Commission approved its sale to the Valley Electric Association, an electric cooperative serving Pahrump and Amargosa valleys; the power was generated at Hoover Dam. Service with Valley Electric began with 194 customers in Beatty and 6 in Rhyolite.

There was no community sewer system in Beatty as of 1949; nearly everyone had a septic system. Eventually there were so many septic systems that the groundwater was becoming contaminated. In the 1970s, a sanitation district was formed to put in a community-wide sewer system.

Communication with the rest of the world was late in coming to Beatty. A telegraph line served the town while the T&T was operating, but when the railroad shut down the line was removed. Fairly early during World War II, phone lines were strung from Las Vegas. Crowells' fluorspar mine, deemed an essential industry by the federal government, helped Beatty get a high priority, AA-1 rating, for the installation of phones.

But even in the late 1940s, it was still quite difficult to reach people in Beatty by phone. There were only two public phones: one in Brownie's Store, which was closed in the evening, and another in front of Azbill's Store (formerly the Revert Mercantile), where street noise and the phone's distance from homes made it difficult to use. A campaign was begun for installation of a public phone that would be "readily available at all times for both incoming and outgoing calls." By the late 1950s, there were approximately 30 phones in Beatty. In about 1960 a modern dial phone system was installed.

Beatty did not have electricity until the late 1930s, and for many years the town had only one street light. Unidentified person is pictured examining the solitary light pole. Date of photo is unknown, but it first appeared in a May 1956 article on the Revert brothers in Minute Man Magazine, *a publication of the* Union Oil Company. Nye County History Project—Revert Collection

Grace Davies, a long-time resident of Beatty, with a bobcat her husband, Fred Davies, trapped in 1938. Nye County Town History Project—Reidhead Collection

*Joe Andre operated a drugstore in Beatty that featured a soft drink and ice cream fountain.
Unidentified woman seated at Andre's Fountain, circa 1935.* University of Nevada, Las Vegas—Dickinson
Library Special Collections

*Joe Andre's Silver Diner Cafe and Drug Store located at the corner of Second and Main,
diagonally across from the Exchange Club, 1938.* University of Nevada, Las Vegas—Dickinson Library Special
Collections

Four young women residents of Beatty, early 1930s. Left to right: Lorraine Thomas, Babe Palsgrove, Chloe Colvin Lisle, and Florence Phinney. Nye County Town History Project—Lisle Collection

Children playing in snow, Beatty, circa 1939. Central Nevada Historical Society— Reidhead Collection

Caesar Strozzi (circa 1940), a native of Switzerland and a long-time resident of Beatty, came to the area at about the time of the Rhyolite boom. Strozzi was married to a local Shoshone Indian woman and raised a family in Beatty. His descendants still reside in the community. The family operated a small farm in the Grapevine Mountains, northwest of town. Nye County Town History Project—Gillette Collection

Pioneer Educators

In 1937, Ert Moore, a young schoolteacher, came to Beatty looking for a new job. His first position in Nevada, which he had held for two years, was at Deerlodge, an isolated area about 30 miles east of Pioche in Lincoln County. In 1937, when the enrollment fell to two students, Lincoln County closed the school. Hearing that teachers were needed in Goldfield and Beatty, Moore and his wife set out for Ely, then Tonopah, "over unpaved roads across sandy stretches when the car running boards would drag on the sides of the ruts." They arrived in Goldfield only to find that the last vacancy had been filled. They hastened on to Beatty and found there was a vacancy.

Moore taught in Beatty for five years before moving to Gabbs in 1942. While he was employed in Beatty, Moore and his wife lived in a three-room miner's house that had been moved there from an abandoned mining camp, possibly Rhyolite.

The elementary school consisted of two rooms and toilets, and four grades were taught in each of the two rooms. This building was old but very sturdily constructed. The high school building consisted of a one-room structure brought in from some old mining camp. The dimensions of the building were about 12' x 20' and there

Beatty schoolteachers and students, 1938. Back row (left): teacher Fred Dees, responsible for grades 5–8; (second from the left) teacher Chloe Lisle, responsible for grades 1–4; (standing in front of the flag pole) principal Ert Moore, responsible for grades 9–12. The tall boy with glasses in the back row is Robert Revert, son of Albert and Henrietta Revert; Johnny Cobb is the tall boy standing on the right of Revert. Front row (far left): Dewey Ishmael, son of well-known Nye County resident George Ishmael; (second from the left) Bombo Cottonwood. Jack Crowell, son of J. Irving, Jr., and Dorothy Crowell, is the blonde boy in the striped shirt in the front row. Nye County Town History Project—Lisle Collection

was only one door. Heat came from an oil stove near the door, and the stove was between the students and the exit. . . . Playground equipment consisted of one backstop and goal for basketball for the older students and nothing for the younger ones to play with (Moore, 1979:19).

In 1938, Fred Dees was hired to teach the upper grades. Dees was a mature and experienced teacher, and even today his former students speak fondly of him and credit success in college to the excellent education they received in his classes.

The Beatty Indians During the 1930s

During the 1920s and 1930s, there was an Indian camp in Beatty located on the east side of the railroad tracks, sheltered in cottonwood trees along both sides of the river. The majority of the approximately 15 families living there were Shoshone; they represented bands from throughout western Nevada and eastern California, including Death Valley, Lone Pine, and Bishop. Some came from as far away as Elko. Their homes were makeshift and had no plumbing. Water was carried in buckets from an outlet across the tracks belonging to the railroad (T. Cottonwood, 1987; Gillette, 1987).

Prior to the Depression, many of the Indians worked for the railroads that served the area and some helped construct Scotty's Castle. In the 1930s, a high percentage were employed by the Works Progress Administration. When that program ended and the railroads folded, the community disbanded and members did not return. Indeed, the camp was usually deserted during the summer as families went their various ways to cooler areas. Some visited relatives; others would migrate to camps in the surrounding mountains. For several weeks in the fall, beginning in late September, the Indians in the Beatty area were involved in harvesting pine nuts.

Conclusion

Between 1920 and 1940, Beatty was the economic hub of a vast area stretching from Sarcobatus Flat in the north to Ash Meadows in the south and from Death Valley on the west to the Lincoln county line on the east. Although the town experienced little growth, residents were able to earn their living by working for the railroad, owning and working in local business and small mining operations and being employed in local and state government. It was a friendly community—everyone knew and respected each other. Still very much isolated, in many ways Beatty remained a small frontier town. Except for the automobile, it was scarcely indistinguishable from many communities found in the American West fifty years earlier.

The Revert Brothers' Union 76 gas station, located on Main Street, Beatty, 1957. The local gas station served as a social center. In the days prior to television, many men would often go down to the gas station to visit with friends and neighbors and pass the time. Leaning on the hood of the car is Robert Revert; Norman Revert is leaning against the wall of the station; Art Revert is visible in the background in a white shirt, and next to him with his back to the camera is Red O'Leary. Nye County Town History Project—Revert Collection

CHAPTER SIX

From World War II to 1960

The period from World War II to 1960 was a time of transformation for the town of Beatty. Though the total population changed little and the town's physical appearance remained relatively the same as it had been prior to the war, economic changes took place that would significantly impact the community's future. With the exception of Crowells' fluorspar mine, whose product was judged necessary for the war effort by federal authorities and thus remained open, the government's closure of gold mines in the area during World War II brought a permanent end to underground mining throughout the Beatty area.

Coinciding with the demise of underground mining came the increased and permanent presence of federal defense-related activities in the local economy with the establishment of Nellis Air Force Range in 1940 and the Nevada Test Site in 1950. Moreover, the establishment of Death Valley as a national monument in 1933 and Nevada's legalization of gambling in 1931 set the stage for the emergence of the town as a tourist center. Although tourism's impact was slow to develop, the town became increasingly oriented around servicing automobiles and providing food and lodging to highway travelers and the ever-increasing number of visitors to Death Valley. The rapid emergence of Las Vegas as a world-renowned tourism center was a major stimulus to Beatty; Beatty became a tiny tourist satellite to the glamorous city. Through it all, however, Beatty remained a small town, one in which face-to-face social relations prevailed, where serious crime was rare, and where people cared about each other.

Growth and Change After World War II

The population of the Beatty area nearly tripled between 1930 and 1950. In 1929, the population was 169. By 1940, the population of the Beatty township, extending from Springdale to Lathrop Wells, was 450; some of the growth was the

For a time during World War II Ralph Lisle and his partners lived in the old ghost town of Panamint City in the Panamint Mountains on the west side of Death Valley. They worked a tungsten property out of Panamint City and used burros to transport supplies in and tungsten ore out. Ralph Lisle with two of his burros on the trail to the mine, about 1942.

Left to right: Bill Martin, Ralph Lisle, Philip Lisle (Ralph's brother), and Sam Colvin (Ralph's brother-in-law), with burros in the Panamint Mountains, about 1942.

result of mining activity at Carrara. Beatty weathered the Carrara shutdown, following the bombing of Pearl Harbor; in 1950 the population was 485.

Beatty experienced many changes during and after World War II. At the outset of the war, the federal government shut down all of the gas stations in town except for the Union Oil outlet; it also closed down all nonessential mining operations, which included gold and silver mines. Because fluorspar was essential in the production of steel, the Crowell Mine was allowed to operate; in fact, production was expanded. The war led to a severe shortage of manpower in Beatty. Many able-bodied men volunteered for military service and others were drafted.

In October 1940, more than a year before Pearl Harbor and the official entry of the United States into World War II, the U.S. government established the Tonopah Army Air Base and the Las Vegas Bombing and Gunnery Range (later renamed Nellis Air Force Range) on a vast area of land east of Beatty. Weather stations were placed around the range. Though there were a number of productive grazing, mining, and homestead claims on the newly restricted area, its closure did not represent a large economic loss for the town of Beatty. However, it was more than a decade before action was taken by the Air Force to compensate individuals for the privately owned lands and mineral and grazing rights that had been reserved for the 3-million-acre Las Vegas Bombing and Gunnery Range in Nye, Clark, and Lincoln counties. Prior to compensation most of the land had been leased by its owners to the Air Force for $1 a year or a similar nominal figure.

When the war was over, most Beatty residents expected life to return to

This building, known officially as the Old Town Hall, was the social center of Beatty for many years. The Old Town Hall was originally constructed in Rhyolite, where it served as the Miners Union Hall. After Rhyolite folded it was moved to Beatty to the corner of Third and Montgomery streets. It was a well-constructed building made of huge timbers and featured a ceiling lined with pressed tin. To the regret of many, it was torn down in the 1960s. University of Nevada, Las Vegas—Dickinson Library Special Collections

normal. It never did. Mining in the Beatty area did not return to its pre–World War II level, and the era of the small, underground mine ended forever. The deathblow had been dealt during the war: Scrap metal was very valuable, and mines that had been closed were scavenged for their track, pipe, engines, hoists, and compressors. Large machinery that was too heavy to move was dynamited and broken into smaller pieces. Most of the mines had not been highly profitable to begin with, and any effort to reopen them following the war necessitated a reinvestment in track, pipe, and machinery, which could not be justified. In addition, men were no longer being trained as hard-rock miners, and in time, fewer and fewer men had the skill and knowledge to operate small, underground mines.

Motels: Beatty Puts Out the Welcome Mat

During the 1930s there were few accommodations for tourists or travelers in Beatty. The old Gold Ace Bar had a few rooms but they were mainly for the bar's hired help. The same was probably true of the Exchange Club. The Montgomery Hotel, the finest hotel in the Beatty region, had long since been moved to Pioneer. There were a few accommodations available at the Beatty Hotel and across the street at the Mayflower Hotel.

The first modern motel in Beatty, El Portal, was built at the west end of town on the road to Daylight Pass by a man named Jim Staley in the late 1930s. Originally El Portal was an auto court with rooms and adjoining garages, but the garages were later converted into rooms. Prior to the construction of El Portal, travelers who broke down on the highway or were otherwise stranded often stayed with local families until repairs could be made.

In 1947 and 1948, there was a great deal of building and improvements in Beatty's accommodations. In April 1947, Charles H. Dodge of Grand Rapids, Michigan, opened his "ultra modern" Gateway Trailer Park at the north end of town on land purchased from the Reverts. A month later plans were announced to add seven new units to El Portal, whose name had been changed to the Bullfrog Motel. In 1948, the Bates family purchased the Bullfrog Motel, and the original name (El Portal) was restored ("Bates Family Purchases Spacious Bullfrog Motel," 1948). That same year Dodge sold the Gateway to Bid Porter, former owner of the Cook Ranch; and ground was broken by V. E. Elliot of Long Beach, California, for a 12-unit motel—the Wagonwheel—at the junction of Highways 95 and 58, where the Gold Ace had stood before it burned down.

Some years after El Portal was built, Hank Melcher built the Amargosa River Inn (originally called Hank's Motel) at the corner of Beach and Main—the former site of a small Standard station just south of Richings' store. The Burro Inn, Stagecoach, Lori Motel, and Brockmans' Desert Inn (which was built along Highway 95 approximately across from the Burro Inn) are all of more recent vintage.

The California Hotel located on Main Street in Beatty; date unknown (probably early 1930s). The California, originally known as the Mayflower Hotel, had been moved to Beatty from Pioneer. Later it was converted to apartments, known as the Cobb Apartments; it burned down in 1972. Nye County Town History Project—Palsgrove Collection

Accommodations in Beatty during the 1930s were spartan by today's standards. The Beatty Auto Court, known locally as the Yellow Cabins, was situated on the west side of the Amargosa River channel on the northern approach to town. Nye County Town History Project—Lisle Collection

Beatty was the closest community to the site where tests of atomic weapons were conducted at the Nevada Test Site beginning January 1951. Newspaper headlines from the Beatty Bulletin, a supplement to the Goldfield News, provide an interesting record of nuclear testing activity as it was reported locally. Included here are samples of three headlines from the Beatty Bulletin spanning the years 1951–1953. Nye County Town History Project

The Nevada Test Site

In mid-January 1951, the Atomic Energy Commission (AEC), predecessor of the U.S. Department of Energy, announced that atomic tests would begin on the 5000-square-mile bombing and gunnery range located directly east of Beatty. The Nevada atomic experiments, it was announced, were being designed to "save precious time" in perfecting atomic warfare, including "experimental nuclear explosions for the development of so-called A-bombs." Tests related to the development of atomic warheads for artillery shells and guided missiles were among the chief objectives ("Beatty Appears to Be Nearest Town ..." 1951). On January 27, 1951, an atomic weapon was first tested over Frenchman Flat.

To many Beatty residents, the tests were more of a curiosity than anything else. The shots were usually set off early in the dim light of dawn, and many locals gathered at a site southeast of town to watch them. The sight of an atomic explosion in the first light of dawn is remembered as thrilling by some Beatty residents. One instant there was darkness; the next second there was blue-white light. The light rapidly expanded and then contracted to almost nothing. Then the orange fireball started to build, the colors faded into purples, and the huge mushroom cloud formed. Usually there was no sound except for a faint rumbling, like thunder, in the distance.

Beatty is generally upwind from the test area, and radiation fallout from testing has never been seen as a concern in the community as it was for residents more likely to be living downwind from ground zero, such as those in Railroad and Reveille valleys to the north, Alamo in the Pahranagat Valley in Lincoln County, and St. George, Utah, to the east. Moreover, Beatty residents have been trustful of the government on nuclear matters, and the majority believe that their trust has been justified. Most admit decades later that they are much less naive regarding nuclear testing than they were in the early years of Test Site operation. The vast majority of Beatty residents said they see no real harm in the community from testing.

One hundred nuclear devices were detonated in the atmosphere at the Nevada Test Site between 1951 and 1958. Tests included drops of "bombs" from high-flying aircraft, hurling of an atomic missile from a 20-ton cannon, and testing of the effects of a nuclear blast on a "typical" city especially constructed on the Test Site for the experiment. Between November 1958 and August 1961, a testing moratorium was in effect between the United States and the USSR. Testing resumed in 1961 when the Soviets violated the agreement. All nuclear testing moved underground at the Nevada Test Site when the Limited Test Ban Treaty was signed on August 5, 1963, in Moscow. Since then more than 500 underground tests have been conducted, with minimal dispersion of radioactive contaminants into the environment beyond the Test Site.

(Above) Many miners who worked in the tunnels in Rainier Mesa resided in Area Camp 12 on the NTS, circa 1980. (Below) Sedan Crater on the NTS was formed by the explosion of a 100-kiloton atomic device on July 6, 1962. The crater is 1280 feet in diameter. Both photos: U.S. Department of Energy

After the signing of the Limited Test Ban Treaty in 1963, all testing by the United States at the Nevada Test Site was moved underground. For underground tests, large vertical shafts were drilled in the desert floor and tunnels were mined into mesas. Atomic devices were detonated in these holes. In this photo, taken at Rainier Mesa, workers are shown preparing a tunnel for a test. Miners secure the tunnel walls with long bolts and epoxy to prevent the walls from tumbling in during a test. Nye County Town History Project—U.S. Department of Energy

Signal cables laid out at a test location on Yucca Flat, Nevada Test Site, Nye County, Nevada. These cables will be attached to a nuclear device lowered down a borehole. The cables will relay scientific data to recording trailers at the surface. The borehole is beneath the tower, which will be removed prior to detonation of the atomic device. Nye County Town History Project—U.S. Department of Energy

Economic Benefits of the Nevada Test Site

Employment opportunities at the Test Site resulted in an influx of new families into Beatty beginning in 1951. As a result, housing was at a premium. A number of Test Site families moved to Beatty and sent their children to the local schools. Rents in Beatty, despite the housing shortage, were said to be lower than in Las Vegas. Local businesses reported a noticeable increase in sales. There was talk of an access road between the Test Site and Springdale on Highway 95 and also of a railroad spur line to the Test Site with a right-of-way passing through or near Beatty. Through the years a small number of Beatty residents have been employed at the Test Site.

The presence of the Test Site has meant contracts for a few Beatty businesses. Beginning in 1951, the Revert brothers operated the first oil distributorship on the Test Site; they supplied petroleum products to the federal government and also to Test Site contractors. Robert Revert remembered his efforts—in the days when he was in charge of site security—to have workers who lived on the Test Site buy Nye County automobile plates. His success added to Nye County's slim tax coffers (R. Revert, 1988).

Another benefit to Beatty and to Nye County is the contribution made to the tax base by contractors working on the Test Site. Prior to the 1960s Nye County was poor; funds were always short. A lawsuit instituted in the mid-1960s by Nye County and supported by Clark County and finally won in the Nevada Supreme Court in 1970 (spearheaded by Nye County District Attorney William P. Beko) forced contractors working on federal property to pay county taxes (R. Revert, 1988; Neighbors, 1988).

With money from the taxes, the county has been able to undertake many projects that previously had been impossible. Nye County, for example, used part of the money to pay cash for the construction of a high school in Pahrump. Over the years, Test Site contractors have also made available to nearby communities and groups considerable amounts of surplus equipment at minimal charge. For example, much of the electrical and plumbing supplies used in the construction of Beatty's Water and Sanitation District and in local park and recreation projects originated as surplus equipment on the Test Site.

An aerial view of Yucca Flat, Nevada Test Site, showing the many pox-shaped depressions scattered across the valley; each depression marks the site of a previous detonation of a nuclear device in a borehole. Nye County Town History Project—U.S. Department of Energy

The Revert brothers, sons of Albert and Henrietta Revert. Left to right: Norman, Robert, and Art. Main Street, Beatty, 1956.

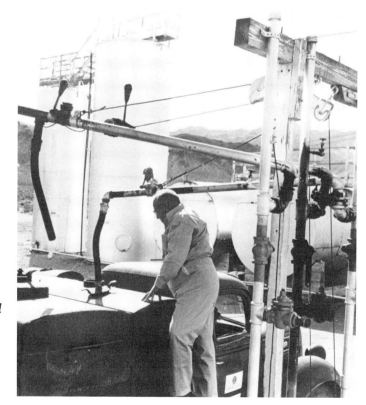

The Revert brothers served the NTS with petroleum products during the first years of the facility's operation.

Conclusion

In 1960 Beatty was the largest community in Nye County south of Tonopah. Though it had become a part of the modern defense and tourist economy, it remained very much a frontier community in its values. Residents of Beatty might earn a living by working at the Nevada Test Site or by owning a gas station, but when it came to how they looked at the world, they probably had more in common with a Rhyolite prospector or miner than someone living in a similar-sized community in many other areas of the country. Then—as now—residents of Beatty loved the desert and its vastness; the town's geographic isolation, far from being a disadvantage, was seen as a precious asset. Residents took pride in their honesty and their desire to treat others as they wished to be treated—with fairness and dignity. Though they were dependent on the economic system that stretched far beyond Beatty, they cherished their independence and freedom from the rigidity and demands for conformity that other small communities outside Nevada often imposed.

Because the Nevada Test Site has been closed to the public for more than four decades, it has become a wildlife preserve for a variety of animals, including centipedes, rattlesnakes, bats, golden eagles, and wild horses. U.S. Department of Energy

An aerial view of Beatty, circa 1980, prior to the development of the Bond Gold Mine and the influx of many additional workers and their families into the community. Nye County Town History Project—Sullivan Collection

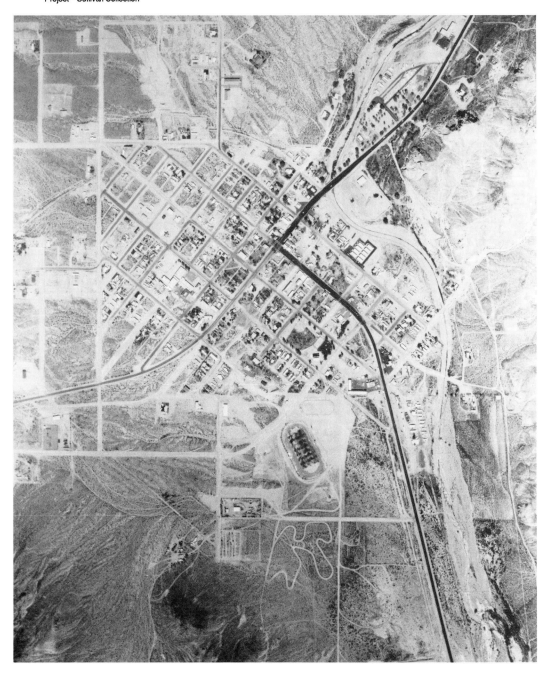

CHAPTER SEVEN

The Modern Era: 1960 to the Present

Beatty's infrastructure developed significantly in the early 1960s. New community sewer and water systems were constructed; new power lines brought electricity from Hoover Dam; and a new phone system was installed. Additionally, a spirit of modernism and community participation led to cooperative activities that benefited the entire community.

The Beatty Volunteer Fire Department

As in small towns everywhere, Beatty residents live with the threat of fire; in Nevada, however, the dry climate increases the threat. From the time the town was established through the 1950s, wooden structures that caught fire almost invariably burned to the ground.

Beatty's first fire station, a building constructed of galvanized tin, was located on the north side of the Old Town Hall on Montgomery Street. Beginning about 1961, a group of young, community-spirited residents decided to push for better equipment and training for Beatty's volunteer fire department. The new firehouse was made from cement blocks purchased by the county, mortar left over from the construction of Scotty's Castle, and other materials scrounged from the Test Site. It was built by volunteer labor. In 1970 when Nye County won its suit regarding taxing contractors at the Test Site, money from that suit bought a fire engine for the new firehouse. Constant pressure was successfully applied on the Nye County commissioners to acquire additional fire-fighting equipment.

The volunteer ambulance service was eventually incorporated into the fire

In March 1987 the second floor of the Exchange Club caught fire. Thanks to the quick response by Beatty's well-trained and well-equipped Volunteer Fire Department the building suffered only minimal damage and was soon reopened for business. In previous years, prior to the development of the community's high-quality fire-fighting force, many structures were completely destroyed by fire. Nye County Town History Project—Reidhead Collection

department, and the Fleischmann Foundation contributed to the purchase of an ambulance. By the 1980s, the Beatty fire department was an efficient force. Buildings that in the past would have burned to the ground are now regularly saved. In a major fire in the Exchange Club, for example, in the winter of 1987, damage was limited to the upper story because of the effectiveness of the fire department.

Civic Improvements

Prior to the 1960s, Beatty lacked recreational facilities. What served as a "ballfield," an area of gravel and rocks, was the result of attempts to scrape the sagebrush off one corner of a lot. With no adequate field, students at the Beatty school could not play tackle football. There were limited options for children and adults who wanted to swim. They could splash in the cold water of a rancher's reservoir in Oasis Valley or travel to the Beatty Narrows, where there were some small natural pools. Aside from a small swimming pool at one of the local motels, the closest facility was at Renee Gibson's place above Springdale or in Death Valley, 40 miles away.

In 1965, community activists, led by Jack Crowell, decided to remedy the situation. They formed a Parks and Recreation Advisory Board and informed the

Nye County commissioners of their desire for more recreational facilities in Beatty. The board's efforts eventually produced results: Two ball fields and a large swimming pool were constructed.

Schools, Medical Care, and Churches

When the Reverts moved to Beatty in 1930, young Robert attended school with the other children in an adobe building located behind the Exchange Club. During the 1930s, building materials were salvaged in Rhyolite and transported to Beatty, and a schoolhouse was constructed between Fourth and Irving on Montgomery Street, the site reserved for a school on the original plat map of the town. The building was still in use in 1991. Several other structures were added to form the school complex, including the old high school building. In the late 1950s and early 1960s, after two rejections by the voters, a bond issue for construction of additional school space was passed, and buildings to house an office, three classrooms, and the gym were added. Additional buildings were constructed in the late 1960s, and still later six more classrooms were constructed and a prefabricated building was assembled to serve as the shop and dressing room for the gym. In 1991, a new multi-million dollar high school was built for students from Beatty, Amargosa Valley, and Death Valley. The old school buildings are now used by children from kindergarten through the eighth grade.

For many years there was no medical care available in Beatty; the nearest physicians were located in Tonopah, more than 90 miles to the north, and Las Vegas, more than 110 miles to the south. One resident remarked, "Read the newspaper. They talk about a poor town some place in the Midwest that is 16 miles from a doctor. In rural Nye county, when you're 16 miles from [health care],

Beatty Episcopal Church, Main Street, Easter Sunday, 1941. Nye County History Project—Palsgrove Collection

Members of the Beatty Lions Club, 1959. Meetings were held at the Atomic Club (later the Burro Inn). Over a period of many years, members of the Lions Club came together to perform worthwhile community services. Central Nevada Historical Society

you're close" (J. and M-K. Crowell, 1987). Doctors could be consulted over the phone after telephone service became available during World War II, but prior to that residents were extremely isolated from medical care.

Rural Nevadans as a group have never been noted to be strongly religious. Yet for many, church and religious services have always played a vital role in their lives. It is not known exactly when the first European-based religious services were observed in Beatty, but it was certainly in the community's earliest days.

The Episcopal Church, a stone building on the corner of Third and Main, is the oldest religious structure in Beatty; it dates to a period prior to the 1920s. Beatty's Catholic Church was built in 1956 on Main Street between Third and Fourth. Father Sidney Raemers and military personnel in the area at the time are reported to have been the driving force behind the construction of the Catholic Church. It has always had mission status, and a priest from Tonopah holds services twice a month.

Formation of the Lions Club

Old-timers in Beatty remembered that for a short time in the 1930s, the community had a Lions Club. In 1959 a new Lions Club with over twenty members was chartered. Members of the Tonopah Lions Club, including Joe Friel and Roy Wolfe, helped establish the Beatty club, which met every Monday night in the basement of the Exchange Club for dinner and to plan charitable activities, including raising money to help poor people in the area receive eye care and eyeglasses.

Because Beatty lacked a chamber of commerce, the Lions Club also assumed typical chamber activities. Members of the club answered letters from individuals

One of the most important and well-received activities of the Beatty's Lions Club were the burro races, held annually during the 1960s and early 1970s. Rules required that contestants place a halter and pack on a wild burro and then lead it over a pre-established course. The contestant in the photo represents Tonopah's newspaper. Central Nevada Historical Society

around the country who desired information on Beatty, and they worked closely with chambers of commerce in Tonopah and Las Vegas. Jack Crowell, the Lions Club's first president, remembered that the organization also served as a social club for the town. It helped community members meet each other and provided a basis for get-togethers.

Burro races, one of the Lions Club's most interesting activities, began in 1961 and lasted for twelve years. Burro races were held on Armistice Day and coincided with the forty-niners' annual celebration in Death Valley. It proved to be a very popular three-day affair—in fact, too popular. When the burro races became more widely known, the events began to attract rowdies from other areas, and for too many people the affair became a three-day drunk. In 1972 the races were discontinued because many townspeople reluctantly concluded that the rowdies and drunks, who had come to dominate the affair, were bad for the community's image and safety, and their presence negated the event's benefits.

Tourism

After the 1940s, tourism slowly emerged as one of two dominant features in the community's drive to survive and grow. (The other feature was the defense-related employment at Nellis and the Nevada Test Site.) Beatty was well positioned to capitalize on the postwar growth of tourism. It is located in the heart of the last great flowering of the Old West in America and is also one of the gateways to Death Valley, which was granted national monument status on February 11, 1933. The emergence of nearby (by Nevada standards) Las Vegas as a world-class tourist destination was an additional factor.

The growth of tourism in Beatty can be clearly seen for one period following World War II in figures from the old *Beatty Bulletin*. In 1944, 55 vehicles a day came from the north into Beatty. Between 1948 and 1949, traffic over Highway 95 increased substantially, with 206 vehicles a day coming from the north in 1949 compared to 109 the year before; more than half had out-of-state license plates. In 1949 an average of 48 cars a day came into town over Daylight Pass. In that same year, a total of 440 cars entered Beatty daily compared to 336 the year before. In 1954, the annual encampment of the Death Valley Forty-Niners was expected to draw 10,000 people.

In recent years, recreational vehicles have further increased the importance of tourist travel in Beatty's economy. More and more older Americans have become nomadic. They live in campers or motor homes and travel about the

Frank and Edith Brockman moved to Beatty in 1957 and constructed the Desert Inn Motel at what was then the far south end of town. Since then, there has been a steady growth in the number of motel rooms and RV parking spots available to travelers wishing to vacation or spend the night in Beatty. Such growth is testimony to the vital role tourism plays in the modern Beatty economy. Nye County Town History Project—Brockman Collection

country as they wish. In the 1980s, additional RV facilities were developed within Beatty and on its outskirts. Tourist travel in and out of Beatty tends to be heaviest from Washington's birthday until about Easter or Mother's Day. Motels are heavily booked during this period. Of particular importance during this season are the "snowbirds"—seminomadic citizens who leave the northern areas of the country during the winter season to take advantage of the warm weather in the Southwest. When the weather turns hot, the snowbirds migrate back north.

From Waitress to Blue-ribbon Businesswoman

Jane Cottonwood spent her early childhood in the eastern United States. Then her family moved to Los Angeles for several years, and Jane attended school there. In 1949 the family decided to move to the desert. While attending school in Tonopah, Jane met Ted "Bombo" Cottonwood and later they were married. In 1951 the newlyweds returned to live in Beatty, where Bombo had grown up. For many years Jane worked long hours as a waitress at the Exchange Club and across the street at the Wagonwheel Restaurant (J. Cottonwood, 1987).

The Cottonwoods had two daughters who became 4-H members when they were older; Jane became a 4-H leader. She was pleased when the girls became interested in horses. They loved to participate in horse shows, especially gymkhana, which involved games on horseback such as barrel races. Soon Jane was putting on a horse show in Beatty each year during the first week of May.

Hosting horse shows opened a new world for Jane. Winners of contests were awarded ribbons and trophies, which Jane had to purchase. One day when she was discussing the difficulty of obtaining ribbons with the owner of Trophies of Las Vegas, Jane commented, "I don't think it's such a big thing; anybody can make those ribbons."

"Gee," the owner replied, "I wish you could." This conversation started Jane thinking. Perhaps she could make her own ribbons. She took some ribbons apart on her kitchen table to see how they were made and confirmed her suspicion that they would be easy to manufacture. She thought about this project off and on for a couple of years (J. Cottonwood, 1987).

One day in 1967, she mentioned the idea to a friend who was an accountant. He offered to invest $4000 to start Jane in the ribbon-making business. Thus began Janda Ribbons—a business venture that is a dream come true for Jane Cottonwood as well as an American success story.

In her small house in Beatty, Jane began making the ribbons in the living room and printing letters on them in the master bedroom. She sold her first orders to Trophies of Las Vegas and soon obtained a contract from people who were putting on a fair in California. The living room and bedroom became cluttered with ribbon production, and Bombo offered to build her a "factory." He constructed a 16-x-20-foot building next door to the house and, as Jane said, "He has never quit building to this day." Since the construction of the first garage-sized building, Jane Cottonwood's ribbon factory has grown room by room. The 16-x-20-foot addition that Bombo originally constructed did not suffice for long.

Dolores "Dolly" Gillette, a native of Beatty and long-time employee of Janda Ribbons, shows a few of the many types of ribbons produced by the company. Nye County Town History Project—McCracken Collection

He soon built a 16-x-30-foot addition and then added a 10-x-50-foot trailer for the manufacture of trophies. When the operation outgrew the trailer, he added a 24-x-55-foot building. At that point the Cottonwoods moved out of their home and built a new one; the business now occupied their old home. Thus, the manufacturing facility grew by modules, with each module constructed by Bombo (J. Cottonwood, 1987).

For several years, Janda Ribbons has been a major employer in Beatty. There were 30 employees in the summer of 1991, with 24 to 26 working during the off-season. The number of peak-season employees is down slightly from a few years ago because of increased automation. Jane is proud that most of her employees are highly skilled and have been with her for years.

For many years, most of Janda Ribbons' clients were in the western United States—California, Nevada, Arizona, Montana, Texas, and Oklahoma, but now Jane does business throughout the country and has even expanded into New Zealand.

Asked the secret of her success, Jane replied that she always has had a lot of energy; she worked hard as a waitress and is working just as hard, if not harder, now. Price and product quality are vital to her business achievements, and she is optimistic about future growth.

Sign at the entrance from Highway 95 to the Beatty low-level nuclear waste dump operated by U.S. Ecology, 1990. The dump is one of three such facilities in the United States. Nye County Town History Project—McCracken Collection

A Low-Level Radioactive Waste Storage Facility

A low-level radioactive waste disposal facility, operated by U.S. Ecology, is located several miles south of Beatty near Highway 95. The facility, which began operating in the early 1960s, provides a steady source of employment for a dozen or so families in the area and further strengthens the community's pioneering role in the development of nuclear technology.

Beatty residents regret that the facility has become something of a political football in recent years. As with the Nevada Test Site, few people in the community complain about the site or its method of operation. Most believe that the operators of the facility have been good neighbors. U.S. Ecology has made numerous donations to community projects, including the fund for fire trucks and an annual scholarship to a graduating senior from Beatty High School. Moreover, the company often lends its heavy equipment when the community needs it (for example, a cherry-picker crane was needed to raise and decorate the community Christmas tree and a grader was needed in the construction of the ballpark).

The Proposed Yucca Mountain Repository

Since the U.S. Congress passed the Nuclear Waste Policy Act in 1982, there has been a great deal of activity by the U.S. Department of Energy to determine the geotechnical suitability of Yucca Mountain to be the nation's first high-level

An aerial view of Yucca Mountain, located on the southwest boundary of the Nevada Test Site, not far from Beatty, 1982. Nye County Town History Project—U.S. Department of Energy

nuclear waste geologic repository. Yucca Mountain is located approximately 15 miles southeast of Beatty, Nevada, on land controlled by the federal government. The facility must be designed to safely isolate large quantities of highly toxic and dangerous nuclear waste from the human environment for 10,000 years, and the DOE will not know if the location is suitable until site characterization is completed around the year 2000 (Bradhurst, 1991).

If the site is judged to be geotechnically suitable, the DOE must then receive a permit to construct and operate the proposed nuclear waste repository from the Nuclear Regulatory Commission. Under even the most optimistic scenarios, it is not expected that a repository would be operational until the end of the first decade of the twenty-first century.

Late in December 1987, the U.S. Congress passed legislation that amended the 1982 Nuclear Waste Policy Act in order to single out Yucca Mountain as the prime candidate site for storage of high-level nuclear waste. Supporters of the 1987 amendment feel that the government's singling out Yucca Mountain for the possible storage of high-level nuclear waste is proper given the area's aridity and sparse population, the large amount of nuclear testing that has taken place at the

Nevada Test Site over more than 35 years, and the necessity of restricting the area for thousands of years to come regardless of future waste storage projects.

Those opposed to a nuclear waste repository at Yucca Mountain point out that there is a big difference between the relatively small levels of waste produced through nuclear testing and the large amounts planned for storage. They argue that most nuclear waste is produced in the eastern United States and that Nevada has done enough for the country with the atomic testing program and its many military installations. Moreover, they fear the unknown problems such a facility might present.

A Caring Town

Although Beatty is a small community not known for its wealth, it has the reputation, of which the residents are very proud, of being a caring town. As Chloe Lisle said, "Over the years many people have put themselves back into the town." Bert Lemmons agreed: "I have seen here in town, periods where you could shoot a cannonball down Main Street and you wouldn't hit anything but a sleeping dog. You wouldn't think there was a hundred dollars in the town. But [if somebody has] a tragic accident, see how quick, within an hour or so, there's a thousand dollars or so which has been raised. Yes, I've seen it happen many a time" (R. and C. Lisle, 1987).

Beatty, the frontier oasis, continues to grow.

Nye County Town History Project. Montage by Polly Christensen

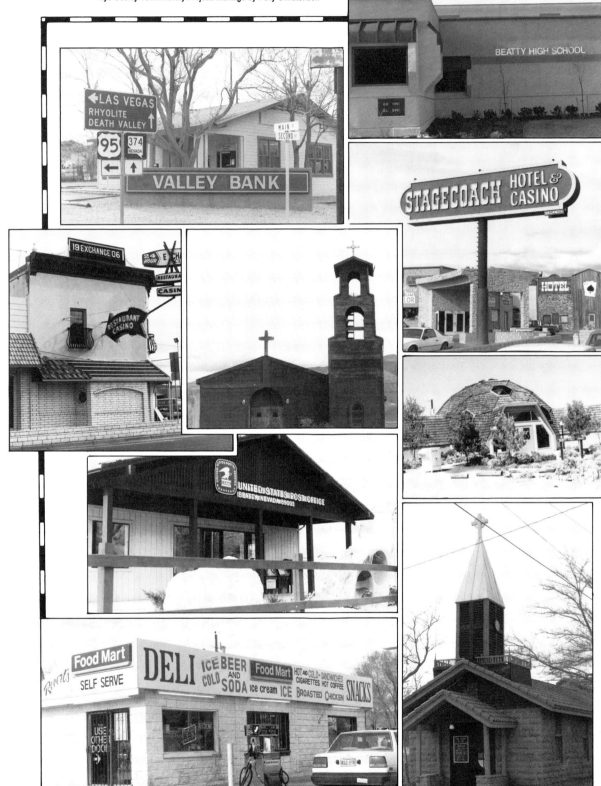

CHAPTER EIGHT

The Future

Beatty residents feel that the community had been fortunate over the years in having been spared the boom-and-bust economy that characterizes so many other communities in the rural West. They point out that even during the Rhyolite boom Beatty remained relatively small; Rhyolite's collapse left Beatty to survive and grow on its own. Over the years growth was slow and sporadic. Yet in 1930 Shorty Harris prophetically noted:

> There was plenty of gold in those mountains when I discovered the original Bullfrog, and there's plenty there yet. . . . Stock speculation—that's what killed Rhyolite! The promotors got impatient. They figured that money could be made faster by getting gold from the pockets of suckers than by digging it out of the hills (Harris, 1930: 20).

Then Harris made a prediction: "If the right people ever get hold of Rhyolite they'll make a killing; but they'll have to be real hard-rock miners, and not the kind that do their work only on paper" (Harris, 1930:20).

New Mining Techniques

Shorty Harris had no way of knowing that it would take advances in technology to make his prediction come true, but true it proved to be, nevertheless. Advances in gold and silver refining and extraction chemistry involving the use of a weak cyanide solution in "heap leaching" in the late 1960s and early 1970s enabled modern miners to economically operate on gold and silver ores that run as little as .02 of an ounce of gold per ton—that involves processing 50 tons of rock to obtain 1 ounce of gold (Potts, 1989). (Twenty-five tons of unbroken rock will cover a 17-foot-square area about 2 feet deep.) Such developments in refining

View of Bond Gold Mine near Rhyolite from the top of Ladd Mountain, looking south. The mill is visible in the foreground and the tailings ponds are visible in the background. The milling process is the same one used around the turn of the century in central Nevada. Beatty is about 2 miles to the left.
Nye County Town History Project

The large open-pit mine belonging to LAC Minerals of Toronto, Canada. The pit is on the east side of Ladd Mountain. Nye County Town History Project

technology meant that gold miners no longer had to restrict themselves to narrow seams of ore that meandered through rock formations beneath the earth's surface, first appearing and then disappearing unpredictably. Miners no longer had to engage in the expensive and dangerous labor of drilling, blasting, mucking, tramming, hoisting to the surface, sorting, and milling only the most select portions of a gold-bearing block of ground. With heap leaching, large portions of a geological formation—in some cases an entire mountain—could be blasted, hauled to crushers on trucks large enough to carry a locomotive, then placed on leaching pads where a weak cyanide solution circulated over the crushed rock leaches out the gold and silver. By the late 1980s, heap-leaching technology had transformed the gold mining industry in Nevada: The state produced more than half the nation's and 5 percent of the world's gold. Much of the latter-day gold boom in Nevada was centered on old mining camps, where entire mountains into which old-time miners had once tunneled were being removed and processed, including Round Mountain in northern Nye County. Several large deposits of gold and silver ores suitable for heap leaching have been found in the Beatty area, and a number of large open-pit mines are either operating or contemplated.

Current Ventures at Ladd Mountain

In 1983, analysis of the fault structure of the district revealed conditions on the east side of Ladd Mountain that were similar to those around the Montgomery Shoshone Mine and the original Bullfrog Mine. Drilling in 1986 and 1987 on that side of Ladd Mountain—not far from where Senator Stewart once hoped to find gold—led to the discovery of an underground orebody estimated to contain 16.4 million tons of mill-grade ore averaging 0.105 ounces of gold (for an estimated total of 1,547,000 ounces of gold) and trace amounts of silver. Aptly illustrating the miner's lament, "so close, but so far," the 1986 drill hole on Ladd Mountain, which first produced an excellent intercept of the newly discovered orebody, was located near an old Rhyolite-era shaft that had missed the ore zone by only 35 feet (Hall, 1989:8–14).

In late 1987 work got under way to construct an open-pit gold-mining operation at Ladd Mountain. First, a feasibility study and operational plan were undertaken. During the peak of the construction phase, a total of 540 workers were employed. To help accommodate the sudden influx of workers, additional mobile home parks were created in Beatty, along with a temporary camp housing 300 people. The first bar of gold from the new Bullfrog Mine was poured July 25, 1989. In August 1989, the permanent workforce totaled 320.

Ownership of the property has changed hands several times over the past few years. LAC Minerals of Toronto, Canada, is currently (1992) the operator and major owner of the property. It is expected that the mine will produce about 240,000 ounces of gold per year during its life, and hopes run high for additional future discoveries in the area.

Beatty's population with the latest mining boom increased from about 1000 in 1980 to between 1500 and 2000 at the end of 1990; if no new mines are brought into production, the population is expected to level off at about 2800 through 1995, then fall again after the turn of the century (Planning Information Corporation, 1988:i). Thus, 80 years after the balloon burst at Rhyolite, Beatty, like so many of its sister communities in rural Nevada, is caught in a boom-and-bust cycle. If the federal government decides to go ahead with development of a high-level nuclear waste repository at nearby Yucca Mountain, activities could pick up the slack caused by reduced mining.

Conclusion

Yet, despite recent growth, the people of Beatty consider their community a fine place in which to live. Most believe that they are fortunate to have lived free from so many of the problems that characterize larger communities. They know firsthand the benefits of life in rural Nevada. As one long-time Beatty resident put it, "We who have lived out in the country like our freedom" (C. Lisle, 1991). Residents of Beatty value a lifestyle still close to the frontier and cherish the values of honesty, personal freedom, respect for the individual, optimism about the future, and a basic "can-do" attitude. They are determined to preserve their present high quality of life (J. and M-K. Crowell, 1987).

References

"Bates Family Purchases Spacious Bullfrog Motel." *Beatty Bulletin*. October 1, 1948.

"Beatty Appears to Be Nearest Town to Site of Atomic Tests." *Beatty Bulletin*. January 19, 1951.

Bradhurst, Stephen T. Personal communication. 1991.

Brooks, Thomas W. *By Buckboard to Beatty. The California-Nevada Desert in 1886*. Edited, with introduction and notes by Anthony L. Lehman. Los Angeles: Dawson's Book Shop. 1970.

Cline, Gloria Griffen. *Peter Skene Odgen and the Hudson's Bay Company*. Norman: University of Oklahoma Press. 1974.

Cottonwood, Jane. *An Interview with Jane Cottonwood*. Nye County Town History Project, Tonopah, NV. 1987.

Cottonwood, Ted "Bombo." *An Interview with Ted "Bombo" Cottonwood*. Nye County Town History Project, Tonopah, NV. 1987.

Crowell, Jack, and Maud-Kathrin. *An Interview with Jack and Maud-Kathrin Crowell*. Nye County Town History Project, Tonopah, NV. 1987.

Crowell, J. Irving, and Dorothy. *An Interview with J. Irving and Dorothy Crowell*. Nye County Town History Project, Tonopah, NV. 1987.

"District Loses True Friend in Death of A. M. Johnson." *Beatty Bulletin*. January 16, 1948.

Dye, Tom. "Gold Rush Heading Toward Las Vegas." *Las Vegas Review-Journal*. March 19, 1989.

Egan, Ferol. *Fremont, Explorer for a Restless Nation*. Garden City, NY: Doubleday. 1977. Reprinted by University of Nevada Press, Reno. 1985.

Elliott, Russell R. *Nevada's Twentieth-Century Mining Boom: Tonopah, Goldfield, Ely*. Reno: University of Nevada Press. 1966.

Gillette, Dolores "Dolly." *An Interview with Dolores "Dolly" Gillette*. Nye County Town History Project, Tonopah, NV. 1987.

Hall, Robin G. *Bullfrog District: A Second Boom*. Denver: Bond Gold Corporation. 1989.

Harris, Frank "Shorty." "Half a Century Chasing Rainbows." *Westways*, pp. 12–20. October 1930.

Lingenfelter, Richard E. *Death Valley and the Amargosa: A Land of Illusion*. Berkeley: University of California Press. 1986.

Lisle, Chloe C. Personal communication. 1991.

Lisle, Ralph F., and Chloe C. *An Interview with Ralph F. and Chloe C. Lisle*. Nye County Town History Project, Tonopah, NV. 1987.

Moore, Ert A. *Experiences of a Pioneer Educator*. Reno, NV: Reno Oral History Project. 1979.

Murray, Tom G. "Letters from a Death Valley Prospector." *Desert Magazine*, pp. 8–11. June 1963.

Myrick, David F. *Railroads of Nevada and Eastern California*. 2 vols. Berkeley, CA: Howell-North Books. Vol. 1, 1962; Vol. 2, 1963.

Neighbors, Roy. *An Interview with Roy Neighbors*. Nye County Town History Project, Tonopah, NV. 1988.

Planning Information Corporation. "Community Development Report: Town of Beatty, Nevada." Prepared for Nye County Board of Commissioners by Planning Information Corp., Denver, CO. August 1988.

Potts, Donald B. Personal communication. 1989.

Revert, Arthur. *An Interview with Arthur Revert*. Nye County Town History Project, Tonopah, NV. 1987.

Revert, Robert A. *An Interview with Robert A. Revert*. Nye County Town History Project, Tonopah, NV. 1988.

Ritter, Betsy. *Life in the Ghost City of Rhyolite, Nevada*. Terra Bella, CA: Terra Bella News. 1939. Reprinted by Sagebrush Press, Morongo Valley, CA. 1982.

Rocha, Guy Louis, "Rhyolite: 1905–1940: An Historical Overview." In *Nye County History Project Historic Property Survey*. Tempe, AZ: Janus & Assoc., Inc. 1980.

"Scotty Buried on Hill Near Famed Castle." *Beatty Bulletin*. January 8, 1954.

Weight, Harold, and Lucile. *Rhyolite, Death Valley's Ghost City of Golden Dreams*. San Francisco, CA: Calico Press. 1972.

First house in Beatty, 1906. National Park Service—Death Valley National Monument

About the Author

Robert D. McCracken, a descendant of three generations of hardrock miners, was born in the high country of Colorado, where he lived until he was eight. His love for Nevada and its people began in the 1950s when he and his brother helped his father operate mines at several sites in Nye County, including Reveille Valley and Silver Bow. During his college years, McCracken worked in Nye County on construction jobs. He earned his Ph.D. in cultural anthropology at the University of Colorado and has taught at Colorado Women's College, California State University at Long Beach, and UCLA. He is the author of numerous scientific reports and articles and was cited in *Time* for his work on human evolution. In 1981 he and his daughter, Bambi, returned to Tonopah, where his father had retired. He began the Nye County Town History Project in 1987.

Books from Nye County Press

by Robert D. McCracken

A History of Amargosa Valley, Nevada (cloth)
ISBN: 1-878138-56-1

The Modern Pioneers of the Amargosa Valley (paper)
ISBN: 1-878138-58-8

A History of Beatty, Nevada (cloth)
ISBN: 1-878138-54-5

Beatty: Frontier Oasis (paper)
ISBN: 1-878138-55-3

A History of Pahrump, Nevada (cloth)
ISBN: 1-878138-51-0

Pahrump: A Valley Waiting to Become a City (paper)
ISBN: 1-878138-53-7

A History of Tonopah, Nevada (cloth)
ISBN: 1-878138-52-9

*Tonopah: The Greatest, the Richest, and the Best Mining Camp
in the World* (paper)
ISBN: 1-878138-50-2

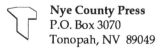

Nye County Press
P.O. Box 3070
Tonopah, NV 89049